Short Skirts and Shorthand

Secretaries in the 1970s

by Sarah Shaw

First published by Lulu Press Inc., 2020

ISBN 9781716802140

Copyright © Sarah Shaw, 2020
All rights reserved.

No part of this publication may be reproduced, stored in a retrieval system, or transmitted in any form, or by any means, without the prior permission in writing of the author, nor be otherwise circulated in any form of binding or cover other than that in which it is published and without a similar condition including this condition be imposed on the subsequent purchaser.

Some names have been changed to protect privacy.

Cover photo of Amanda Lunt in 1978 © Sarah Shaw

Contents

Introduction..5

Chapter 1 : Something you just became........................11

Chapter 2 : A day in the life...48

Chapter 3 : Temperatures, typewriters and subversive trousers. .82

Chapter 4 : A wife without the love.............................110

Chapter 5 : The sexy secretary....................................142

Chapter 6 : The secretarial trap...................................174

Chapter 7 : The job carousel......................................203

Chapter 8 : A history of the future….....................……. 235

Acknowledgements..261

Bibliography..263

Introduction

In 1971, according to the UK national census, approximately three-quarters of a million British women were employed as secretaries, shorthand writers and typists. They worked in every form of business, public and private. They kept government, businesses, councils, hospitals, banks, the media, manufacturing and agriculture running because, at the time, there was no other way that correspondence could be exchanged, reports and contracts prepared, products distributed and marketed and records of transactions retained. They performed a million and one miscellaneous chores supporting the men (and they were usually men) for whom they worked, from fetching cups of coffee to taking minutes of meetings. These thousands of women, hammering typewriters, scribbling shorthand and organising the hell out of offices were promoted, appreciated, ignored, patronised, harassed and dismissed. Their work was barely understood by others and often went unrecognised, yet it was the engine that kept all the wheels of administration in motion.

If you were to try to imagine a secretary, what do you see? The elegant and poised Miss Moneypenny yearning after James Bond? A chirpy blonde in a miniskirt? The feisty trio from the film *Nine to Five?* We have seen secretaries on TV and in the cinema, in newspaper cartoons and cheap romances. We know who they were and what they did. Is there anything more to say about them? I think there is, and that this book reveals a world that was far more interesting, varied and challenging than popular representations suggest.

Why have I limited its scope to the 1970s? Three reasons. First, it was the decade in which assumptions about gender divisions at work were more widely challenged, with women demanding equal opportunities with men and feminists singling out the role of secretary for particular criticism. Second, it was the decade when automation began to displace the model of the boss and his secretary that had survived for nearly a century. Lastly, somewhat fortuitously, my own years working as a secretary were between 1970 and 1979.

*****

It was at an event for *The Secret Diary of a 1970s' Secretary*, my diary for 1971, that I was approached by two older women who were delighted that someone had, at last, written a book about what it was like to have worked as a secretary, although that hadn't exactly been my intention. This intrigued me. I felt sure the subject must have been covered already. As it turned out, during the 70s there was an interest in secretaries in academic circles which spilled over into the women's pages of newspapers, but since then little has been published about them.

Early on in my research, I discovered Dr Rosalie Silverstone's thoroughly-researched and informative PhD thesis, *The Office Secretary* (1972). This has never been published commercially but is available online[1]. It was an invaluable resource, especially because she includes quotations from interviews and survey results carried out at the time. I was especially honoured to meet Dr Silverstone at the initial stage of planning this book to discuss with her the issues I wanted to explore and am extremely grateful to her for permission to quote from her thesis.

However, this book is not an academic study. It's for the general reader, for anyone who unwound the end of a paperclip to pick the inky fluff out of a letter 'p' on a manual typewriter; for their bosses, especially those who weren't quite sure what their secretaries did all day, and for readers with a general interest in that turbulent decade, the 1970s.

I have tried to give the most accurate picture possible of secretaries' working lives using a mix of personal memoir and quotations, set within the historical context. The quotations were compiled from responses to a set of questionnaire-type memory prompts distributed to branches of the University of the Third Age and retired staff at companies such as the BBC and IBM. More than 50 online replies were completed, to be rounded off with ten personal interviews. This left a daunting amount of material to be edited into a readable account, and I must apologise to those whose contributions could not be included for reasons of space alone.

I confess that the book contains a large proportion of responses from London, particularly from former BBC staff. However, I would suggest that this doesn't invalidate its content because a large number of secretaries worked in London, and the BBC was a significant public service employer. I was delighted to be able to include material from a few former secretaries from the United States, Canada and New Zealand too.

A few content warnings. While the improved opportunities for, and attitudes at work towards, women today were universally appreciated by contributors, a significant minority were critical of feminist views now considered mainstream. Allowing them to speak for themselves has resulted in the inclusion of opinions which may seem controversial or outdated. These have not been included in order to provoke, but simply to ensure that all points of view are represented.

Another risk I have taken is to refer to the person to whom the secretary was directly responsible as the 'boss', even if it today it is a questionable term. This is because it was the most commonly used description at the time and one with which contributors were most familiar. Also, for the sake of simplicity, I have assumed that all secretaries were female. This wasn't so, but fewer than 5 per cent of UK secretaries were ever men. I apologise to any male secretaries reading this book. Despite my best efforts, I was unable to track down any of you. (I did at one point think I had captured one, only to receive a somewhat diffident email from a gentleman who assured me he had *definitely* been an 'Assistant,' and never a secretary, despite the person who had shared an office with him assuring me otherwise.)

The book is arranged so that the first chapter explains how young women became secretaries; the next two and the penultimate chapters describe the everyday world in which they worked: their routines, processes, use of pieces of equipment and so on. As far as I know, these have never been described before by those who carried them out, so it seemed important to record this information in, I hope not too laborious, detail before it is lost forever. The middle three chapters look at more general issues using popular stereotypes: Chapter 4 explores relationships between the boss and secretary through the image of the 'office wife'; while in Chapter 5 a second image, that of the dolly bird, leads to the subjects of sex and sexual harassment. Chapter 6 considers feminist criticisms of the secretarial role and how the women themselves fared when attempting to move into other spheres of work. In these three chapters, comparing what was said or written at the time with the contributors' experiences yields some surprising results. The last chapter explores the changes brought about by office automation and includes contributors' reflections on the past.

*****

Before we head back to the 70s, it's worth understanding how and why secretarial work had become women's work.

It didn't begin like that. 'Secretary' is a word that goes back to the fifteenth century. Originally it defined a man employed by a king or person of high standing who handled his correspondence, record keeping and other business — literally the person who dealt with his secrets — and for this the utmost discretion and skill in etiquette was essential. You may remember from history lessons, or from Hilary Mantel's Tudor trilogy, that Thomas Cromwell was a secretary, first to Cardinal Wolsey and then to King Henry VIII; not the first, or the last, secretary with a boss who left him in charge of the office while he went off carousing with his mates.

Secretarial posts remained a masculine preserve until the latter part of the nineteenth century, by which time bureaucracy and administration had expanded significantly. Young British men who would have looked to clerical work as a career, like Bob Cratchit in *A Christmas Carol,* had set off in large numbers to seek their fortunes in the Empire or the Americas. This left a surplus of unmarried, middle-class women for whom the only respectable occupation on offer was that of governess. With so many applicants for every post, wages fell to pitifully low levels and activists such as Josephine Butler stepped in to campaign for more opportunities to be made available to them. The Civil Service and the Post Office were the first to respond by recruiting female clerks. Despite objections to the mixing of the sexes and concerns about the capability of women to perform such work, the trend continued, especially when companies realised that women could be employed more cheaply than men. By the time of the 1871 UK census, there were well over a thousand female commercial clerks.

In the mid-1880s the small-arms company Remington succeeded in refining previous models of the typewriter to manufacture one which was easier to use and cheaper to produce. Now documents could be typed, i.e. printed, more quickly than a clerk could write them in longhand, and they were easier to read. Women, at first themselves called 'typewriters', were ideal users of these new machines, the work was not only just like housework, repetitive and ideal for neat little fingers; but also, because it was so new, any concerns voiced by male clerks could be dismissed by claiming that it was an entirely new occupation. Meanwhile, Isaac Pitman had been experimenting with different forms of writing in shorthand, bringing them together to form one which was simple to learn and use. By studying this system, using his pioneering correspondence courses, single, middle-class girls were able to learn typing and shorthand at home and to seek secretarial employment. It thus became a popular choice of occupation; it was respectable, well paid, offered good conditions and the possibility of working for someone of importance. There was also the prospect of moving on to more responsible roles, for example, supervising other secretaries, or becoming a teacher of the skills in one of the newly opened colleges. Best of all, it gave these women a degree of financial independence.

The model of the shorthand and typing secretary working for her boss persisted for nearly a century, with the general assumption that the young woman would perform this work for a few years until she married and then, supported by her husband's income, would leave paid employment to become a housewife. Even if she returned to office work later on, it would be on a part-time basis and for 'pin-money'. Such an arrangement neatly avoided upsetting any societal apple carts. While men started at work in junior administrative positions expecting to rise up through the company, women were expected to content themselves in support roles to them, both at work and at home, performing the repetitive routines which they wished to avoid.

So let me take you down to a world where, on cold mornings in high-ceilinged houses, gas fires hiss. Where footsteps echo on uncarpeted floors, and the smell of spirit wafts down the corridor from a duplicating machine. Where the air is thick with cigarette smoke. Where war widows sit in a room at rows of desks, deafened by the clatter of typing, typing, typing. Remember: be helpful, pay attention to detail and don't be too clever, or the men won't like you.

Chapter 1 : Something you just became

In the 1970s, the process of becoming a secretary had changed little since the beginning of the century. A reasonably well-educated girl was trained in typing and shorthand, possibly adding other subjects such as a foreign language or bookkeeping, and once she had achieved an acceptable level in these skills and had the certificates to prove it, she was slotted into a job commensurate with her education and social background.

In August 1969 I opened an envelope with my A-level results and realised that my plan to go to university was dead in the water; but, as I had little idea about what studying there would be like or whether I wanted to go anyway, it felt more like a merciful release than a disappointment.

What was I to do instead? Like most middle-class young women at that time, I had been brought up to assume that my goal in life was to find a husband, marry and 'settle down'. Career guidance had been totally lacking at school, and as for motivation ... well, nobody had suggested I should be 'not average but awesome' as a current exhortation goes. Frankly, being average was pretty much what I wanted, anything else was dangerous. So, being a conventional sort of girl, I assumed the time between my leaving school and getting married would be spent in the genteel pursuit of young men while supporting myself doing a respectable job. In practice, this meant selecting an occupation from a choice of three: nurse, teacher or secretary.

Nursing meant dealing with blood, bandages and bed-making. Too much responsibility. Crossed that one off. Teaching meant dealing with children. Slightly better. But after a fortnight's volunteering at a kids' holiday club I realised I didn't like them much. Crossed that one off too. What was left was 'secretary'.

I knew nothing about secretaries other than what I had seen in films, where they perched behind desks adjusting their coiffures, answered intercoms and waved the hero off to adventures somewhere else. So I asked my stepmother, herself a retired secretary, what was involved. Her answer had something to do with typewriters, but there was no mention of sick people or screaming youngsters. So far, so good. Then, she added that learning shorthand and typing would be 'useful. After that,' she continued, 'you can sit those A-levels again if you like, or (with a meaningful look) get a job and earn your living.' I asked my best friend, already working as a secretary, for her opinion. She replied (with another meaningful look) that the job was so easy *anyone* could do it. I asked my father if he would pay my college fees and train fares. He said yes. And that was it.

Not the most carefully constructed career path, and you might imagine I was unusual in taking this path so haphazardly, but was this so? Let's find out.

Throughout this book I am going to bring in reminiscences from other former secretaries, building a picture of 70s' secretarial life. So let's begin by seeing how they went into the job.

Deirdre Hyde
Northwood, Middlesex

'My parents came from Ireland in the 1930s as economic migrants, I was one of five children. My father worked on the land, we lived in a tied house so there wasn't much money. My mother worked at night, cleaning factories. She strongly believed in education, without it being shoved down our throat. We all went to good schools on scholarships. Our fares were paid for, which was just as well because my brothers went to schools in Ealing and Finchley.

'You got your O-levels and then you got a job; there wasn't any "What do you want to do?" discussion. It was either nurse or secretary, not teacher because that meant college. Or, because we were Catholics, a nun. There was no talk of my going to university, as a family we did not know the map of privilege. What mattered was a safe job and, a respectable means of earning one's own living. My father had a saying, 'You go to work to earn money to buy bread to give you strength to go to work'. And it's true.

'A secretary was not something I chose to do, as in "When I grow up I want to be a ....", it was something you just became. I knew nothing about what it entailed, other than you worked in an office, for a man mostly, typing letters which he had dictated to you. I knew no one who was a secretary.'

Sarah Oram
Purley, South London

'I couldn't think of anything else to do. And it struck me and my parents that it was the kind of job that you could do in any area and it might take you on to something else, should you wish it to. You could be a secretary in a publishing office or a computing office or a technical office or an artistic office. But I hadn't a clue about what to expect.'

Even though the new 'plate-glass' universities like East Anglia and York had been deliberately recruiting female students, many parents still considered that tertiary education was for 'other people', especially not their daughters. As one former secretary recalled, her mother had squashed her ambition to go to university by saying, 'Nice girls don't leave home until they get married'. It was much more sensible for a girl to get a job, and in the 70s when there were plenty of vacancies for secretaries, learning shorthand and typing meant you'd never be out of work.

Pam Robinson
Liverpool

'I was an only child, Mum stayed at home, Dad worked as a fitter. I went to an all-girls grammar school. Eight of the girls in my year were from a dockland area in Liverpool, and all our parents were hard-working manual workers who didn't grasp that passing the 11+ was actually the beginning, not an achievement in itself.

'I wanted to be a journalist, so I went to evening classes from age 15 to learn touch typing, and left school a year later in 1969 with four O-levels. I wasn't given very good careers advice. I should've been told to stay at school and take the appropriate A-levels to get into university and on to where I wanted to be, but nobody we knew had been to university, so it was a bit of a mystery as to what you had to do to get there. I'm not thick, but I was mixing with some real high-fliers and there was what I perceived to be a snobby attitude. It was a class thing.'

Jan Jones
North Manchester

'I became a secretary by chance really. My Dad was an engineer by trade, but at the time I was born he and my Mum were running a greengrocer's shop. We lived over it. I was a bright child and did well at my local grammar school but I was never really comfortable there and going to university wasn't something our family did. At least my Mum had the foresight to say that I could only leave at the end of the fifth form if I went to college. She had worked in the local mill and wanted better for me. So then the idea of being a secretary somehow took root.'

Tanya Bruce-Lockhart
South Kensington, London

'I was this over-energetic child, I probably suffered from ADHD but that wasn't defined in the 50s and 60s. Rather sadly, university was never suggested by my mother or my stepfather. I was made to do all sorts of practical things that they thought young ladies should be doing, so I was sent to France to learn French and to the Cordon Bleu School to learn how to cook. Then I wanted to go to the Central School of Speech and Drama, and my mother and stepfather said, "No, you can't because actors and actresses are never in work the whole time." So I ended up at secretarial college. I thought "My God! What's my life going to become?"'

Sue MacCulloch
North London

'It was a nice job that was open to nice girls. It was solid, it had a good reputation. You were in an office, working for a man, usually, and it was just what nice girls did until they got married.'

Another reason for parents to discourage daughters from applying to university was that even after graduating they might still find themselves confronted by the choice of three.

Kathryn Vaughan
West Yorkshire

'When I left school I had absolutely no idea what I wanted to do in life. I only went to university because I loved

Spanish and couldn't bear the thought of having to stop doing it. I had no intention of becoming a teacher as I couldn't face lazy kids messing about with the subject I loved.

'The day after I left Nottingham University with a degree in Modern Languages I went down to London to start a six-month graduate secretarial training course at the City of London College in Moorgate. A friend told me she was going to do it because with secretarial qualifications she would always be able to get a job in London, and I thought it might not be a bad idea. At least it would take care of the next six months and I would be living in London.'

Originally, secretarial posts had been filled by girls with good qualifications, but by the 70s the demand for them in London meant that, while a fifth had passed A-levels and half had reached O-level standard, the remainder came from the non-academic secondary modern schools[2].

Christine Allsop
Chesterfield, Derbyshire

'I attended a secretary modern school. Out of the whole school only one pupil went to teacher training college; the rest of us were told we were not clever enough to go. Being a secretary was really my only option as I was not interested in the others, i.e. hairdressing, nursing, shop and factory work. I did not have high expectations of being a secretary, and I was not disappointed.'

Kathie Hamilton
Brentwood, Essex

'I felt, coming from a secondary modern school, I was just fodder for the office. I had a short interview with a careers adviser who told me it was impossible for me to be a window dresser, which is what I wanted to do, so I should give up needlework, take up shorthand and typing and get an office job — which is what I did.'

Thus far you could be forgiven for thinking that secretaries drifted into the job with little idea of what they were in for, but this wasn't so. There were some very ambitious young women out there too.

Gwen Rhys
South Wales

'I'm conscious that my experience is different from many of my contemporaries, I come from a family of very strong women. My mother (born 1928) went to University and was a teacher, her mother (born 1898) was a businesswoman and owned two shops.

'I went to a girls' grammar school, only 90 girls got in each year from a large catchment area, and after A-levels most went on to university, teacher training or into a bank or post office. While I was at school I made and sold things and was an Avon Lady and a Kay's catalogue rep. I used to arrange trips to Welsh country dances: organise the bus, advertise the event, collect in all the money and make sure that what everyone was charged also covered my own place.

'So when I completed my A-levels in 1971, a Business Studies course was an obvious choice. My school careers adviser would never have thought about it: teaching was what nice Welsh girls did.'

Elaine Day
Forest Hill, South London

'My youthful ambition was to be an astronaut or journalist; why no one encouraged the latter, or even the former, I don't know. A friend had been for an interview at the BBC and decided it wasn't for her. It very much sounded as if it would be for me, as I loved drama, performance and the arts, so I applied for their three-month intensive secretarial course and was successful.

'In those days, if you didn't have a university degree, the way to promotion at the BBC was to start in a junior or trainee position as vacancies were advertised to internal candidates only. Assuming you were successful in obtaining the necessary shorthand and typing speeds at the end of the course, you were guaranteed a job somewhere in the BBC. I was fortunate in being placed straight into television, whereas some girls were sent to personnel or engineering, far from the perceived glamour of production. They didn't stay, they could have been working in any company. What was the point of being in the BBC if you weren't making programmes, was my view.'

Mary Ankrett
Walsall, West Midlands

'I chose this route when I was at school. I was influenced by some of my parents' friends who worked as secretaries. My mother was a busy person and involved herself in little projects such as Christmas and Holiday Clubs, where people would save money weekly. I loved helping her with the book and record keeping. It felt it was important, and that this was something I would be involved in, in an office job.'

Curiously, although the image of a secretary was often of a glamorous, chic woman, this doesn't seem to have been a consideration in choosing the profession — apart from our next contributor.

Hazel Rees
Clapham, Beds

'Up until I was about 15 I wanted to be a teacher. Then a programme came onto the TV called *Compact*. It was set in a magazine office and the editor was called Ian Harmon, who was to my teenage eyes very dishy. His secretary was called Sally, and he married her. No longer keen on teaching, I decided to be a secretary. What an admission!'

*****

Once the decision had been taken, the next step was to learn the necessary skills. In my case, I asked my best friend and learned that she had gone to a private secretarial college in London. We both lived in the Surrey suburbs, so a daily trip into the capital was an exciting prospect.

I ordered brochures from several of these colleges. One was Lucy Clayton's, a college which was not just a place where you learned shorthand and typing but one that would 'finish' you — not kill you off but teach you social graces and etiquette. I thought lessons in deportment (how to sit with your knees together and ankles crossed) dress sense, flower-arranging, cookery and dancing would have finished me off, especially as they advised their young ladies not to display any intelligence, because they would be considered more attractive if they appeared 'innocent and naive'[3]. Putting that one in the bin, I flipped through the other brochures and opted for an institution called Mrs Hoster's Secretarial College, solely because their classes finished an hour earlier than all the rest.

So imagine me on September 22nd 1969. If a bad moon was rising for Credence Clearwater Revival, I had my fingers crossed no trouble was heading my way. The newspapers were filled with stories about 'hippy' squatters being evicted from a posh mansion in London's Piccadilly, and how Merseyside workers had called off a threat to occupy their factory. BBC TV was showing *Z Cars* and *Ask the Family* that evening; cinemas offered *The Italian Job, The Battle of Britain* or Dennis Waterman in *The Smashing Bird I Used to Know.* Leasehold on a two-bedroomed flat in Regent's Park was £7,500. A vacancy for an 'intelligent typist' was advertised at £18 per month while a 'secretary/model with languages and entertaining' could earn just over a thousand pounds a year.

However, I didn't pay much attention to the state of the world that particular day because I had more immediate concerns. Just after 9.00 am, dressed in my best sea-green cord skirt and chequered blouse, I climbed the steps at South Kensington Tube station and found myself in the big city. I walked along Thurloe Place in terror. This was my first day at Mrs Hoster's, and I had no idea what was in store.

On arrival, I was confronted by a wall-mounted clock above a slotted wooden box, between tall racks filled with strips of card. This, I was told, was the clocking-in machine, designed to instil precise time-keeping in Hoster ladies. We should expect to find this machine at our future employers. As instructed, I inserted the card with my name on it. *Bing*! It was stamped. I was 'In'.

Every day at Mrs Hoster's was divided into four sessions of an hour and a half: two for typing, two for shorthand, with a couple each week set aside for other studies, such as accounts and 'office practice'. I could see typing could be useful for letters and song lyrics, but shorthand? My stepmother had mentioned it was a quick method of writing so that a secretary could note down the words dictated by her boss and read them back again when she came to type them out. Wait a minute, I said. My father is an excellent typist. Why don't these bosses type their own letters? 'Because your father is a journalist,' she replied, 'and these other men aren't. It's how it is.'

We learned typing through endless, repetitive practice in a large, high-ceilinged room. About 20 of us sat at old wooden desks behind typewriters that looked like they had been rescued from bombsites, and battered and clattered our way to proficiency. Lesson One was Positioning of Hands, holding our arms parallel to the desk with our fingers pointing down, like pianists, so we could thump the keys from above. We had to do this because the old manual typewriter keys were stiff and heavy, and it was hard to whack them effectively until your wrists and fingers had developed enough strength. So much for those genteel Victorian ladies, I thought. However, when I see today's keyboard users with their flattened wrists resting on laptops, I wonder whether using this position saved us from strain injury later on.

Lesson Two was Insertion (Paper). For this we made a sandwich of plain and thin 'flimsy' paper with a sheet of carbon paper in between them. It was important to get it the right way round as the carbon was inked on one side and you didn't want the print to appear on the underside of the top copy. You inserted this paper sandwich upside down around the back of the roller, rotated it into the typing position, checked it was horizontally aligned and began typing. (Apologies if this is too much detail for you, but remember anyone born in the twenty-first century will probably never have seen it done.) Just as you were about to reach the right-hand edge of the paper, a bell on the typewriter went 'ding!' — like Lady Mary summoning the maid — so you completed the word you were typing and slammed the carriage lever back with your left hand. Thunk!

Then came Lesson Three: Insertion (Ribbon). For this you lifted up the little cover on top, wound the old, worn out typewriter ribbon on to one of the two spools and discarded it. Then you slotted in the juicy new red and black striped ribbon, threaded it through the type guide, cut a tiny hole in it and attached it to the empty spool. Fiddly: and invariably you were left with red and black striped inky fingers. It occurs to me now that, because the black half was worn out long before the red, you really only ever used half of it. The ribbon manufacturers must have made a fortune.

'Touch' typing means typing without looking at the keyboard. First we learned how to locate the 'home keys,' placing our forefingers on f and j with the rest of the hand on the middle row, and repeatedly hitting one, then two, then three fingers, tapping out words like b-u-t b-u-g b-u-m over and over again. Oh, the excitement of reaching the frontiers of z, q, and pesky p, which you had to stab viciously with your little finger to make sure it printed. All the while we had to keep our eyes fixed on the textbook beside us from which we copied the instructions, not that there was any point in looking at the keys anyway because they had been painted over with red nail varnish. It was monotonous in the extreme, but once we had the keys at our fingertips all we had to do was speed up until we reached the gold standard of 60 words per minute (wpm).

'Sugar, ah honey, honey, you are my candy girl ...' The Archies' saccharine hit always reminds me of the rhythmic *clack-clack-clacking* of typewriter keys and the *ting-screech-thump* of 20 slung-back carriage returns. Every morning began with typing to music because maintaining a steady rhythm was essential to gaining speed without jamming the keys. Progress was tested by giving us a page of text, our instructor checked her stopwatch and shouted, 'Go!' and a battery of typewriters fired off until she shouted 'Stop!' and we slumped dramatically in our chairs like exhausted distance runners. The number of words per minute was then calculated by how many we'd typed with a couple of seconds deducted for each mistake.

The second part of the typing course was called 'samples'. Like nineteenth-century maidens exhibiting their embroidery skills, we prepared a portfolio of twenty different types of document, such as various styles of letters, a film script, a set of accounts and a poem, each of which demonstrated a skill such as centring, tabulating or justifying. Errors were not permitted: if you made a mistake you tore out the paper and began again. The Draft and Engrossment of a Will was a particular challenge, it was a lengthy document with a complicated layout for which a carriage accommodating paper 30 inches wide had to be used. It took me three laborious attempts to complete it, in the course of which I decided I stood a better chance of being detained at Her Majesty's Pleasure than of working in a solicitor's office. The idea behind creating this portfolio was that it would be scrutinised by prospective employers but, disappointingly after all that work, no one asked to see mine.

If learning to type meant endless repetition, shorthand required more thought. Armed with our specially purchased fine-nibbed fountain pens, we studied Sir Isaac Pitman's phonetic system. This uses strokes, loops and curves to represent the consonants, with the vowels indicated by the position of the squiggle on, above or below the line. There were other forms of shorthand, but Pitman's was the most common, probably because of old Isaac's astute marketing and the training colleges which were established in his name. We were told that our shorthand should be so accurate that if you were off sick someone else could read your notes and type them back; this always seemed doubtful as I had difficulty reading mine at all.

Pitman's shorthand requires thinking about words by their sound, not spelling. Like many others, I found this difficult to begin with but eventually it fell into place. Pitman's has a cute short form, or special squiggle, for "Thank you for your letter" which is especially gratifying as you can write it faster than anyone can dictate it. The goal we were aiming for was to reach 120 wpm. This was tested by taking down two minutes of timed dictation, transcribing it on to the typewriter, working out how many words had been typed, checking the result against the original passage and deducting two words for every error, and then halving the result. My personal best was 110 wpm, acceptable if not outstanding, but actually it wasn't a problem because I never worked for anyone who dictated very fast. It was only necessary to be able to take down dictation at 130 or 140 wpm if you were going to be a court or parliamentary reporter.

I wasn't happy at Mrs Hoster's. I should have realised it would be very unlike school and that it was a means to an end, rather than an experience to be enjoyed for what it was. Unfortunately I couldn't find any common ground with my classmates, who were a chic bunch of well-dressed young ladies with earrings, make-up and blow-dried hair, and who regarded me, in my Marks and Spencer's twinset, with barely concealed pity. They all had double-barrelled surnames and spoke in that curious, squeezed lemon sort of posh accent about 'Jeremy' and 'Piers', Sandhurst, horses and cocktail parties. Only a few said they intended to find work when they finished the course, I suspect the rest had been parked there by parents to keep them out of trouble, although one girl only put in an occasional appearance as the rest of the time she was on the road with a rock band. I gave up trying to make friends when one Miss Double-Barrel, aghast that I didn't know what a lychee was, handed me a few pennies and ordered me to buy some at a fruit stall so that in future I would know what they looked like.

Even worse, these classmates were incredibly rude to the teachers, treating them as if they were servants from downstairs quarters. But the staff at Mrs Hoster's were immune to this disrespect. They were a tough bunch of Londoners, former secretaries, somewhat frayed round the edges, who were probably as bored teaching shorthand and typing as we were learning them. I particularly liked our shorthand teacher, a Miss E.F. Worster, who had the same Cockney accent and laconic humour as Mrs Alf Garnett in *Till Death Us Do Part*. She punctuated her lessons with little stories, such as one about the time during the Blitz that her neighbour was trapped underneath a bus and it had taken all night to dig her out. One day we arrived in her classroom to find her wearing a 1940s' turban hat, a little odd indoors, but nobody said anything and the lesson began. As ever, she dictated a letter to us along the lines of, 'Our order to you of the 23rd August, number 682 for 2,000 two-inch Coventry bolts has not yet been delivered. Please advise... ' and then suddenly announced: 'I was mugged last night.' She then removed the hat to reveal an extravagant quantity of crepe bandage. Apparently, the previous evening on her way home, she had been hit on the head with a blunt instrument and her handbag snatched by person unknown. Suggestions that the lesson should end at once so she should go home and rest were firmly dismissed. I suppose that in women like her the wartime 'Keep Calm and Carry On' spirit lived on. Maybe a little of it rubbed off on me because despite my unhappiness at Mrs Hosters', I persisted.

The highlight of my day was the lunch break. As soon as I had scoffed my sandwiches and Eden Vale chocolate yoghurt, I crossed over the road to the Natural History Museum, where Dippy the Diplocus, or what was left of him, listened to my complaints with the typical resignation of a 150-million-year-old.

He didn't offer any words of comfort, but a dinosaur puts one's troubles into perspective.

Private secretarial colleges like Mrs Hoster's were only one of the institutions where secretarial skills could be acquired. There were far more places for girls at Colleges of Further Education, as these contributors explain.

Jan Jones
North Manchester

'I went to college in Central Manchester to do an OND in Business Studies with shorthand and typing, which was a two-year course. I finished college just before my 17th birthday. Typing accurately has never been a strong point but, after initially finding Pitman's shorthand impossibly hard, it suddenly clicked into place and myself and another girl streaked away. I gained 140 words per minute shorthand and was encouraged by my teacher to go to further study and become a court reporter.

'However, the training for that took place in Hyde, then still in Cheshire. In 1969 it was somewhere I had only vaguely heard of and didn't altogether know where it was. It would have meant a bus journey into central Manchester and then another bus or train journey out to Hyde. I wasn't a particularly adventurous or confident young lady at that time. It was all a bit too hard for me to contemplate.'

Gwen Rhys
South Wales

'I wanted to do a Business Studies degree, but they were very new then and I wasn't sure if I would like the academic work, I'm a practical person. I found a course at the College of Commerce in Hull which offered a HND in Business Studies combined with Secretarial Qualifications. Twenty girls were on the course. We all had good A-levels, we were all interested in business. Half the girls had a European language at A-level and they also did secretarial studies in that second language.

'I LOVED the course. Gained a distinction in my HND, Distinction in RSA Stage III Typing, 120 wpm shorthand and the Private Secretary Certificate of the London Chamber of Commerce.'

Some FE College courses added non-secretarial subjects to their curriculum, presumably to extend the girls' education and make it more attractive, foreign languages being a popular extra.

Amanda Lunt
Epsom, Surrey

'I went to the Holborn College in Red Lion Square, which specialised in law, languages and commercial studies. Since I seemed to have a talent for languages I embarked on a secretarial course including, apart from the usual office skills, commercial French and German and A-level Law. I soon decided that commercial languages weren't really for me though I found the law course interesting and almost considered staying on to pursue a law degree.

The most risible part of the course was "Secretarial Duties", which had its own written exam of which the opening question entailed describing in the most mundane detail how to begin your day, literally hanging up your coat, checking out the diary of your boss (always known as your "chief") and making him (of course) a cup of tea. At the end of the year, we were treated to a talk by a beautician on cosmetics and skin care, a rather gushing lady who was at pains to inform us that "a woman's hands should be soft".'

Margaret Taylor
Northolt, Middlesex.

'My father was a London bus driver and in the early 1970s London Transport Executive operated a scheme whereby they sent you on a six-month secretarial course to a London college (not only did the company pay the college fees but also paid you a salary whilst you were there). At the end of the training you would be offered a position.

'I attended Kingsway College of Further Education, Kings Cross, London. There was a number of secretaries trained by LTE in this way, and I remember girls employed by other companies being in my class, particularly a couple of girls sponsored by Trusthouse Forte. We studied shorthand, typewriting and a subject called "secretarial duties". These lessons were in the afternoons. For our morning studies we were able to choose any topics we were interested in, I studied psychology, English language and literature, and art.'

Jenny Mustoe
Aylesbury, Bucks

'I wanted to work in agriculture, my very middle-class parents wanted me to be a secretary/ marry the boss. Sitting in the dentist's waiting room one day, I read an article about the only two-year farm secretarial course leading to an OND in Business Studies (for farm secretaries) at Aylesbury College of Further Education in Stoke Mandeville. Seemed like the perfect compromise.

'It was a fantastic two years, lectures all day every day and often extra ones in the evening, so we really had to work hard. Great fun driving tractors, learning about machinery, helping out with the pigs, cattle and sheep as well as picking potatoes.'

Secondary modern schools taught typing as part of their curriculum for girls; grammar schools offered it as an extra option, along with shorthand, in sixth forms. One grammar schoolgirl signed up for evening classes and found herself back at the same desk she used during the day. Then there was the Sight and Sound Centre in London which offered a kind of instant typists' course, and whose ads I remember being plastered all over London Tube trains.

Catherine Preston
London

'No shorthand for me, I was going to be an audio secretary! That was the future, or so I thought. So I learnt to type at the Sight and Sound Centre. This was in a gloomy room above a shop in Oxford Street. One hour a day for eight days. Huge screen in front of possibly 40 typewriters with blank keys. We placed our fingers on the middle row as instructed and then looked at the screen. A key with letter would light up and we would copy. Gradually we worked around the whole keyboard to know which fingers went to which keys and then it was just a matter of picking up speed. Kind of brainwashing. Very effective. I think I left with about 30 wpm. My father paid, so no idea how much it cost.'

It wasn't just school and college leavers who became secretaries. Refugees from the other two choice of three occupations were also channelled in that direction by staff at Training Opportunities

Schemes (TOPs), government funded courses for women wanting to change career or return to work after having children.

Terri Kaye
London

'Initially I was a physiotherapist. I hurt my back when I was 32 and had spinal surgery and was told to come out of physiotherapy for a year. So I went for advice, which was not very well given because the lady who was interviewing me kept going to the room next door, where I could hear a man's voice. She was obviously a trainee or something and I thought, Why don't you let me talk to the man directly? She ended up saying secretarial work would probably be the best. I was in London at the time and went for this secretarial course to Pitman's at Wimbledon, I must have had a grant.

'That was an amazingly frustrating six months. Being older probably did make it a bit more traumatic. I wasn't at all good, although a lady that I had befriended very kindly said that my brain was faster than my fingers. I thought having done physiotherapy that probably applied.

'One Friday afternoon I had a really screaming abbadabbjabb fit. Everybody had started going home and I was screaming my head off, saying that if only I was strong enough I'd throw this damn typewriter out of the window. Nobody came to check that I wasn't completely doolally, all the staff just distanced themselves. I felt better for my little screaming outrage, my friend tapped me on the shoulder and said, "Come on, let's go and get the train now", and the typewriter stayed on the desk.'

It was still possible to learn by correspondence course, following the path pioneered by Isaac Pitman.

Diane Jones
South Wales

'I saw an advert in a Sunday newspaper regarding a Vocational Guidance Service which would pinpoint an individual's ideal job. I duly travelled to London to complete three multiple-choice exams, assessing my abilities, interests and personality. I then attended an interview in Harley Street, no less, and was advised that my tests had pronounced that I should become either a writer or a farmer! But since neither of these careers might be viable at the time, and obviously they thought that no right-minded farmer would want to marry me, they advised that I should learn shorthand/typing and become a secretary, wow!

'I immediately bought a portable typewriter from W.H. Smith which cost £12, and enrolled on two correspondence courses in typing and 'speedwriting' [another form of shorthand] which I then followed up with a secretarial course at a local college.'

It's an interesting point that although there were many places in the UK where secretarial skills could be acquired, the level of achievement expected was far short of that demanded by employers in other countries, as Rosalie Silverstone discovered when she interviewed this secretary from Sweden.

'One secretary who was educated in Scandinavia in a 'Handelsgymnasium' (literally "trade school") felt that English secretaries did not receive an adequate training for the job. She had been taught such subjects as international finance, languages to a high standard, economics and law.[4]'

*****

Secretarial colleges guaranteed to find their leavers a job, and so it was that at the end of my nine months' secretarial gestation I was told to visit the Placements Officer in her office at Mrs Hoster's. I found a sharp-faced woman sitting at a desk piled high with manila folders. Selecting one, she scanned it briefly.

'You look like a country girl. D'you like horses?'

'Not much,' I replied. I spent most of my time indoors reading, writing and playing the guitar, so nil points for perception there.

'Oh, I thought you seemed the outdoor type. There's a vacancy at Lord's Cricket Ground working for the MCC.'

Ah! Handsome young men in white flannels! This sounded excellent.

'Oh no,' she corrected herself hastily '– that's gone. What are your interests?'

'Music.'

She peered into another file and ran her finger down a page. Was this my chance to meet the Stones? She turned the page. Badfinger? Not Gilbert O'Sullivan surely, I had standards.

'There's a vacancy here for a secretary at Ibbs and Tillet, they're a classical music agency. Might suit you.'

She arranged for me to attend an interview at their offices in Wigmore Street. Off I went. Emerging from the underground at Oxford Circus I spied Broadcasting House in the distance, rising majestically against a bright blue summer sky. So that was the famous BBC: where lived Kenny Everett, Johnny Morris, Betty Marsden, Roy Plomley and all the other voices I knew and loved from radio programmes. Wow!

But I was off to meet Mr Ibbs and Mr Tillet, whoever they were. I should point out here that I hadn't quite grasped the purpose of my being interviewed, believing that by having been invited by them I had already been given the job. The interview was so I could decide if *I* wanted to work for *them*.

I had a nice chat with a kindly old gentleman in an office above a record shop for about half an hour. It all seemed most satisfactory, even though he turned out to be a Finance Manager and winced when I guessed the (wrong) answer to a question about percentages. When he mentioned that the job would involve picking up famous maestros at Heathrow Airport, conveying them to the Park Lane Hilton and keeping them entertained, I was delighted to reassure him that I knew how to pour a glass of sherry and was quite accustomed to meeting my uncle off the bus.

Back with the Placements Officer.

'You didn't do very well at that interview, did you?'

Oh! I thought it had gone brilliantly.

'He said you were very inexperienced.'

'Well, I haven't been to work before, have I?'

She looked at me very closely.

'You didn't get the job.'

Brutal, but honest.

'So, where *do* you want to work?'

A moment's pause, as I registered the possibility that this 'getting a job' thing might be more complicated than I had imagined. Then the image of that big white building with the blue sky above it came floating back to me.

'The BBC?'

'Oh for goodness' sake, why didn't you say so?'

She reached for the phone and dialled. 'Doris, I've got one here, she's got the necessary ... [scuffle of papers] ... well it's 110 words shorthand, 50 words typing. No, not 120 words. Anything? Yes. Yes, thank you.'

She put down the phone.

'It doesn't sound very interesting but there is this, something to do with school programmes. Do you know anything about those?'

'Not really.'

'Well for goodness' sake don't tell them that.'

A week later I was Secretary to Assistant (Information and Recordings) School Broadcasting Council, BBC. I later discovered that competition for places at the Corporation was fierce so I had been incredibly lucky to slip in through the Old Girls' network. All that keeping calm and carrying on had paid off after all.

It is ironic that, with so few occupations open to us, when it came to finding a job there was such a wide variety of vacancies on offer. But at least this meant that if your college didn't find you something, there was plenty of choice in the newspapers.

Deirdre Hyde
Northwood, Middlesex

'I remember scouring the *Daily Telegraph* and *Evening Standard* looking for something a little out of the ordinary. And there it was — books, authors, publicity. Oh, and a salary nowhere near that offered by a bank. At my interview, I was asked what my father did.'

Some secretaries were already looking ahead at what the job might lead ...

Sonia Lovett
North London

'In spite of having a music degree from Sussex University I was told that the only way that I could get into the BBC was as a secretary, so I did a postgraduate secretarial diploma at City Polytechnic. That was my way in.

'My first job was in the BBC's Gramophone Programmes Department. They were really pleased because I knew how to spell all the composers' names. I worked on *Desert Island Discs*, opera transmissions, *This Week's Composer* and many other music programmes. It was a good way to learn about the business. My boss had a music degree from Edinburgh, I think, and we were the same age so at the beginning it was a bit galling when he kept asking me to make him coffee. I soon got over that.'

... while for others, plans had to be adjusted as they went along.

Pam Robinson
Liverpool

'I decided to leave school at 16 and do an OND in Business Studies at a nearby commercial college. It was a basic syllabus with shorthand and typing. I thought this would help if I did follow my plan to become a journalist.

'Plan?! I got involved with a fellow student on the same course. Within two months, I was pregnant and we married after knowing each other seven months. Both families (working class) were very supportive, and it was decided that, as my husband would be likely to earn more than me and I had the means with the office skills to earn some money, he would stay on at college and I'd go to work.

'I went along with it as it made sense, I think it's what's known as 'internal colonization'. So when our daughter was 6 months old I found a full-time job as a legal secretary. In 1971 jobs were abundant, you could leave one on a Friday and start a new one on the Monday, no one thought anything of it. In spite of having no previous work experience, I was taken on and stayed there for a year.

'We lived with my in-laws, and my mother-in-law looked after our daughter. She was an absolute diamond of a human being. I owe that woman a lot. She'd had a part-time job which got finished up just before my daughter was born, so she offered to help so that we could get on our feet.'

Carol Brinson
London/Sussex

'My father decided it would be a good idea if I trained as a bi-lingual secretary. Our local College of Further Education was advertising an Advanced Secretarial one-year course, including languages; "Advanced" because it was for people with A-levels, not necessarily any existing secretarial skills. Accepted on course. No languages available after all but I persevered with the secretarial studies anyway. In 1967 I completed the course with moderate success. My grandfather knew someone in the BBC and arranged an interview for me. Failed the tests. Grandfather suggested I gained some office experience by working in his office, the family firm of funeral directors in West London.'

Such was the demand for secretaries that applicants for other vacancies were sometimes diverted to meet it, even someone with medical qualifications, like former physiotherapist

Terri Kaye
London

'I got through without terribly brilliant results, but I did pass. I saw an advertisement for a job at Beecham's Pharmaceuticals. What caught my eye was a job for an Assistant at an allergy clinic so I applied for that. However, their wretched Personnel were a bit too much on the ball. I'd said that I spoke Polish, which I thought would be very useful in that part of London, and they picked up on it and said, "Well, actually the East European Division is looking for a secretary", so that's where I ended up; rather sadly, in my own eyes.'

So far we have only looked at the experiences of young women in the UK, but was the process in the United States similar?

Mary L Cryns
San Francisco

'While in high school I had worked as a sort of secretary at a VA [Veterans Affairs] Hospital. I took one typing class in junior high school eighth grade. We used manual typewriters of course, and the keys were blank because we had to learn the touch system. Although I did not type that fast in the class, I started typing on a Royal manual my Dad gave me at age 14. I'd type stories and song lyrics and such, and loved typing. I became fast without even realizing it.

'In 1976 I graduated from Heald Business College. They had a referral service and sent us out on job interviews. Actually, I went on quite a few because I didn't quite fit the mold of a secretary. I was always the odd-ball of the bunch, kind of a reformed hippie chick in a whole different world.

'I landed a job as a legal secretary with Mullen & Filippi in the financial district, a workers' compensation defence firm. I was terrified because I was assigned to a partner – he was an older guy who looked kind of mean. I was only 19 years old and felt overwhelmed because the office manager showed me piles of files with cassette tapes on top of them. The attorney dictated everything he wanted done on these tapes. I'd learned shorthand in business college, but in the legal field the attorneys had just started using tape recorders to dictate. Cassettes hadn't even come out until I was like seventeen.'

Laurie McGill
Dallas

'Mother was a secretary, and when I was a little girl she gave me her old Gregg shorthand books, and I tried to copy all the squiggles onto a steno pad. I set her bedside table up as my "desk." I taught myself to type in junior high using my mother's Underwood manual typewriter, and when I took shorthand in high school I grew adept at that skill as well, placing first in the UIL (University Interscholastic League) District Shorthand Competition my senior year. I do not recall ever considering any other profession.

'I expected my job as a secretary to be like those seen on television in the 1950s. I clearly remember watching *Love That Bob* as a very little girl and aspiring to be Schultzy, who was secretary to Bob the photographer. There was another 1950s' television program called *Susie,* starring Ann Sothern, Susie was a private secretary to a talent agent. When I started working as a secretary I wasn't disappointed because the job was quite similar to the secretaries depicted on television — answering the phone, typing, taking shorthand, filing. Unfortunately, my bosses were not as handsome as the TV actors.'

For adventurous types, one advantage of becoming a secretary was that you could work almost anywhere with a common language, and during the 1970s London offices were buzzing with young Aussies and Kiwis.

Valerie Docker
New Zealand

'I lived in this small town in New Zealand; no television but read a lot, and most of the books had an English background, so I thought of going to look at some of the places I'd read about. I went to college and learned shorthand, typing and bookkeeping. I worked in an insurance office and at 19 I'd managed to save enough money to get on a ship and I took myself off to England. I don't think I was very unusual, there were other girls doing that. In New Zealand we had this phrase,"Go home to England" for an overseas experience, so that's what a lot of us did.

'My first job was in Wigmore Place, so that was a nice walk from the tube at Oxford Circus through Cavendish Square to this little mews office. The accountants I worked for had a few celebrities on their books. The partners went off to have long lunches and talk about money with them, and that might be when we all might go out for a long lunch at the pub. That was something that really surprised me, because in those years in New Zealand if you had an alcoholic drink during the working day you'd be sacked, whereas it was interesting to see all these people just going off to the pub for half a pint of cider and a scotch egg. It was very relaxed, I thought. Quite novel.'

*****

There was nothing so scary as that first day at work. A fledgling secretary often had little idea about what her future employer did, other than 'sold cars' or 'made chemicals'. She might or might not have had an interview beforehand, she might find herself working for someone whom she had never met. There were so many anxieties: deciding what to wear, how to manage the journey and arrive on time, how to layout the letters, what the shorthand vocabulary would be like, what to say when the phone rang and, most important, locating the Ladies' loo.

My own working life began in an unusual setting. The Langham in Portland Place, just opposite Broadcasting House, had been built as a one London's first grand hotels. In 1889 Oscar Wilde and Arthur Conan Doyle had dined there together. Today, it is a luxury hotel again but, for a few decades in the mid-twentieth century, it was owned by the BBC who, through a process of quick conversion and benign neglect, turned its bedrooms and bathrooms into offices and decanted into it an assortment of useful but unglamorous departments.

Arriving for my first day, I took the lift to the top floor to report to the Personnel Officer and her Administrative Assistant or, in BBC acronym-speak, 'Pers. & AA'. After the experience at Ibbs and Tillet my stepmother had adjusted my interview technique and I had successfully navigated a chat with Pers. a few days earlier. I now knocked on her office door. There was no answer. Pers & AA were not at home. I looked up and down the long empty corridor with its sea-green walls and sea-green linoleum floor, half expecting Jacques Cousteau to snorkel past.

I was early. Ten past nine for a 9.30 start. I waited. It was like the first day at school again, the same sick feeling of apprehension, aware that my life was about to change forever but not able to imagine how. Eventually one of the other secretaries arrived. Having quickly observed that I was a nervous new recruit, she invited me into her office and found me a chair. Remembering my Mrs Hoster's training I asked her straightaway where I could find the clocking-in machine. She was polite enough not to laugh.

Eventually Pers. arrived and I was taken to meet my boss, a middle-aged woman from Tasmania whose job was to deal with the half kilo of correspondence about schools broadcasts that arrived in the post every day. She was exactly the person I needed, a former teacher who was endlessly patient and encouraging. During my first afternoon, spotting that the wastepaper basket was already overflowing with screwed-up paper, she explained it wasn't necessary for me to throw away a whole sheet just because I had made one typing mistake. There was a bottle of white stuff called 'Snopake' in my desk drawer and one of the other secretaries would show me how to use it. A revelation: there had been no talk of Snopake at Mrs Hoster's.

At the end of Day One I went home full of excitement. I had discovered that (a) none of the shorthand phrases I had learned about washers and deliveries was of any use, but instead Pers. had given me a couple of pages of Pitman short forms for words like 'broadcast' and 'television' — obviously it would only be a matter of time before I was asked to select my eight gramophone records and talk about my life on *Desert Island Discs,* (b) rather than using a fountain pen, I could write shorthand with a biro that had 'BBC' stamped on it — groovy, (c) I had a wonderful Adler manual typewriter, a sturdy beast that would be affronted by any suggestion of wearing nail varnish, (d) I didn't have to put full-stops between B B and C as I had been taught, which made typing it easier, and (e) the tea was nothing like as vile as they said it was on the radio. Eagerly I looked forward to the next day.

Later I found out that my first day at the BBC had been a cock-up. I was supposed to have spent it at a staff introductory day, but Pers. had omitted to book a place for me. After a week or so it seemed too late to bother with, so the BBC and I never officially shook hands.

Whichever Pers. had the job of welcoming Amanda Lunt to the Corporation didn't make the same mistake.

Amanda Lunt
BBC, London

'The first day at work for BBC secretaries was the Induction Course, where one was introduced to the

Corporation and its general structure, and to office routine such as use of the Staff List and the correct way to address internal envelopes.

'My first job was in the Secretariat, which consisted of the officials (all male in those days) who minuted the various board and senior management meetings, and drafted replies to correspondence from MPs, government departments and so on. As this was very much part of the inner sanctum of the Corporation I was required to sign the Official Secrets Act (which I don't think I am about to breach!).

'I did find it all pretty daunting, especially as so much of the business was conducted in acronyms and initials, a particular BBC fetish no doubt inherited from the Civil Service, for example the head of Current Affairs Magazine Programmes was delightfully known as 'Head of CAMP'.

'By the end of the first couple of weeks it was clear that I really wasn't up to the volume of work and so was moved to a cosy niche in the Programme Correspondence Section, staffed exclusively by motherly ladies, mainly unmarried, widowed or divorced, dressed in twinsets and pearls and surviving on cups of tea and gossip.'

A major concern for the new secretary was the need to create a good first impression. Secretaries were expected to dress smartly, and look clean and tidy. One new girl had her fingernails inspected on her first day, another was told off for having dyed her hair. You had to smell right too.

Gillian Summers
Bridport, Dorset

'I managed to get a lift with a local fish merchant who needed a driver so he could sleep. The van was full of live fish creaking and squeaking, and very smelly. We arrived at Billingsgate Market at 5.00 am, and there I recovered my suitcase from under a stack of fish. I headed off to a Tube station where I knew there was a good Ladies with room enough to wash and get changed. I had a new winter suit and felt quite smart, at least until I stepped outside and saw all the glamorous fashions trooping up the escalators.

'I walked to Park Street and rang the bell of an imposing front door. No one answered, so I pushed it open to find a small lobby with a notice saying "Wallis Brock – 2nd floor." Up I went and stepped out into a long corridor, at the end of which was a room stacked with great grey metal filing cabinets. I was drawn down that way by the sound of a hoover, and eventually discovered a cleaning lady buzzing her way around. It was just before 8.00 am, the normal time to start work in the Middle East where I had been living, but the cleaner looked at me in amazement and said "Oh, no my dear — there won't be anyone here before 9.30." By the time the junior girls arrived I was feeling very tired, and worried that I might smell of fish.'

The first day could also be a complete surprise.

Sarah Oram
Computing, London

'The job was to do with computing, which I did like the sound of. I thought computers were A Good Thing. It was working for an advisory body to local authorities, which had been set up to find out what computers could and couldn't do for them. In those days, although computers had been around for a while, they took over a whole floor of an office block and did less than your phone does now. So it was a brand-new set-up, new office, new everything.

'The first day was a shambles! It was so new that we had no desks, no phones, nothing. It was like going in through the door into a completely empty office. Everybody was going, "Well we don't know when this is arriving!" "We should get this set up!" But it was the same for everybody, whether you were at the top or the bottom. I enjoyed that.'

Jan Jones
North Manchester

'My first job was as secretary to the Personal Assistant of one of the three Chief Executives. The first day was the first time I met him. He was like a Greek god, which was a bonus. He caused a stir wherever he went. He was tall, at least 6ft, slim, good-looking and with curly blonde hair. He was in his early 30s and happily married, absolutely charming and I really liked him, but funnily I never fancied him: I always go for dark-haired men.'

However, not all surprises were pleasant.

Kathie Hamilton
Brentwood, Essex

'The first day was hell on a stick. It was a six-week trial in a solicitors' office and I was 15, straight from school. Each day the waste bin was overflowing with headed paper full of mistakes — I was so embarrassed I even hid the sheets in my bag. I must have taken home a ream of paper. The supervisor was like a hawk and I think that made me more nervous. I knew I could type and produce a clean letter but found it impossible there, and the more I tried the worse it got. I remember feeling totally inadequate and undeserving of the £5 a week salary. I was afraid and really anxious going in the next day. I was let go after three weeks.'

Heather Pippins
Slough, Berks

'At 13 I went to a technical school, and you did either commercial or domestic subjects. I didn't really see myself sewing and cooking so I did commerce: book-keeping, shorthand, typing and English, as well other subjects. I thought technical school was brilliant because you came out totally employable. I had a very dear friend and she passed to go to the grammar school, but when she came out she wasn't qualified to do anything. She ended up working in a shop, and I thought, well, I've done better than that.

'I had no idea of what being in an office would be like. I mean, you come out of school and you are offered a job, you take it. It was a bit of an eye-opener. I was a very, very junior shorthand/typist/filing clerk for a company that did asphalt for the roads. It was in the grottiest old timber building you can ever imagine, it leaked when it rained. When I used to do the filing I had to put on a pair of wellies to stand in the corridor, the water would be up to here [indicates knee height].

'I stood that for a year and I thought, I don't like this. In the winter time you got the asphalt steaming in the yard outside and you'd get dead cats found in it, and dogs. It was horrible.'

******

Even if we were still wondering how and why we managed it, we had found a job and being there was much more interesting and varied than those tedious hours of practice. And there was the monthly salary to look forward to.

We had much to learn: routines, recalcitrant pieces of equipment, how to forge a good working relationship with the boss and how to avoid that slightly creepy bloke down the corridor.

How we managed, the following chapters will reveal.

Chapter 2 : A day in the life

Office life followed routines, routines that went in cycles. All correspondence, both within and outside a company, was transacted on paper, so every day started with the opening and sorting of incoming mail and ended with the despatch of outgoing. Days of the week were marked by meetings (for the bosses) and deliveries of supplies (for stationery cupboards, photocopiers and vending machines); months and quarters by invoices and statements of company accounts. There were summer holidays to be discussed and planned, and postcards (which arrived after the sender had returned to work) to be affixed to cupboards. Each year as Christmas approached, decorations were exhumed, dusted off and put on display before the annual office party. Dotted around these fixed points were introductions of new colleagues, celebrations for those departing and the regular distractions of office dramas.

Secretarial posts formed a pyramid-shaped hierarchy, the status of each secretary being dependent on the position of her boss within the company. At the top of the pyramid were Personal Assistants (PAs) and senior secretaries, below them multiple levels of general secretaries and shorthand typists. Further down were copy and audio typists, and at the bottom was the typing pool. In small companies this stratification would be much less obvious than in larger, more bureaucratic establishments. Small firms often employed a Girl Friday (named after Robinson Crusoe's servant), a kind of maid of all work, who had to do more or less anything from reception duties to typing letters to buying teabags and cleaning the toilets.

While basic routines were much the same at all levels, the rest of each job differed according to status, the more senior the boss, the greater her responsibility, the more interesting her work and the better her salary. 'Secretary' itself was a loose definition.

Traditionally it implied, as it had for centuries, a confidential assistant to an important person, but had come to denote someone who was capable of writing shorthand. Without that skill you were a typist. But by the 70s these definitions had become blurred and a 'secretary' could be working for more than one important person, or be a typist with a few extra duties thrown in. Further confusion arose when job titles were inflated in order to get round government pay restraints — one woman was given three titles of increasing seniority so she could be paid more while her duties remained unchanged.

A PA worked for a senior manager, perhaps the Chairman, Managing Director or member of the board. having gained experience by working her way up the company. As well as exhibiting the attributes required of all good secretaries: efficiency, reliability, tact and good-humour, she had be completely trustworthy in confidential matters, as well as poised and polite. She assisted her boss not only with his business matters but also with his personal financial, travel and social arrangements, plus any involvement he had with professional or charitable organisations. Her close relationship with him ensured she had a good overview of both the company's business and his private life. Her professionalism affirmed his authority; his status enhanced hers.

Judith Farnell
Yorkshire

'The role of PA was more than a secretary. A secretary was essentially a shorthand typist who might arrange appointments for her boss/keep his diary. A PA works more closely with her boss — organising his diary, arranging travel for him and his guests, preparing documents for meetings, keeping him up to date with office politics (NOT tale-telling or tittle tattle), making refreshments like tea and coffee for visitors or arranging more complex catering for more important guests, filling in for absentee staff (which I did occasionally!) in short, someone on whom the boss can rely to make his/her life easier.'

Sarah Oram
Computing, London

'There was a hierarchy upwards of typists – copy typists – secretary – personal assistant. What you did was, you worked your way up the bosses so you ended up near the top. And when you got there you had a much better idea of what went on. I was a secretary to people who were quite high up. And because I was typing the reports, I could see the correspondence going to and fro, I could see what the business did, and I got involved with everything. It was much more visible.'

Gwen Rhys
Specialist publishing company, London.

'As PA to the Managing Director I was "at the top", everyone treated me with the respect that they treated him. I felt very important, valuable and valued. PAs, especially in small/medium enterprises, undertook the tasks that specialist people do now: facilities management, human resources, travel, health, etc. It was rare for me to leave on time at the end of the day. I would frequently "pp" letters [sign them for her boss] or write them under my own name as PA to him.

'I had a company car. Within 12 months I had a secretary working for me, and by 1976 had also taken on responsibility for the day-to-day running of a subsidiary company. In 1978, when I was 25, I got a 9 per cent company mortgage, so bought a two-bedroom flat in North London. I was never bored.'

Gwen was unusual in becoming a PA so young, generally they were in their 30s or 40s[5]. Other contributors remembered working for old school PAs who were very conscious of their superior position and exacting of their juniors, which didn't always make them popular.

Heather Pippins
Johnson & Johnson, Slough

'I was working in the Company Secretary's office, because then big companies had Company Secretaries, now they don't because they have legal departments. I worked for the Personal Assistant to the Company Secretary. Sitting opposite me was another junior, but she was 18 months my senior, I was the junior junior, the real rookie.

The Company Secretary's PA, she was quite strict which was OK, but she had a go at me one day. "Oh Heather, you'll never get the hang of it." I just looked at her. Even then I was cheeky, I was all of 17, I said, "Yes but at least I have the years to learn, not like some people!" And Helen [sitting opposite] went [jaw drop]. I thought, "Come on, you're not going to keep on talking to me like this, as if I'm down there'.

Wendy Gough
Insurance company, Midlands

'The chief officer's secretary had a lot of power over the junior staff, and policed behaviour and clothing, etc. She controlled the stationery cupboard. I shared a phone with a more senior male colleague and he would appropriate my stuff, such as pens and staplers. The head secretary was very mean to me when I needed more supplies.'

Chris Green
British Petroleum, Feltham

'I remember a Miss Clearly, who was the PA to the head of the research centre at BP. She thought she was much better than us. She told me how to eat my peas, that I should not scoop them up on the fork. I always think about this now when I eat my peas. I'm sure she was very good at her job.'

A PA's day began with checking her boss's office to see everything was in order, perhaps putting fresh flowers on his desk, before she returned to her own office to open and sort the morning's post, and make sure she was ready too. One former PA told me that every morning until she retired she sharpened her 2B pencils ready for dictation. Once the boss arrived, they confirmed diary arrangements and the business for the day. She would take shorthand dictation and transcribe it, and work through other tasks: drafting letters for him, proof-reading a report, renewing his membership of a professional body and sifting through technical journals for articles he might like to read. If necessary she would book appointments, flights and hotels for his trip abroad and type out an itinerary. Then there were her own letters to answer, or to dictate to her assistant, and minutes to take at a meeting. All the while she would be answering phone calls, screening his visitors, putting off any she knew he didn't want to see, and providing the boss and his guests with coffee or tea, perhaps something stronger. However long it took, she stayed at work until he left; she might then accompany him to an evening function. As Gwen said, PAs were never bored.

It was assumed that a secretary with ambition would wish to rise up the ranks and become a PA, but the job didn't appeal to everyone. As one contributor put it, 'I always considered myself a secretary and saw Personal Assistants as women who fawned on the boss, booked his airline tickets, got birthday presents for his wife and wiped his bottom. Ugh!'

At the level of general secretary, the essential part of the job: dictation, typing, filing and phone calls, was the same but with less formality and involvement with the boss's personal matters. Each job was different: some required hours of form-filling, others of telephone work. As it's difficult to describe an 'average' secretary's day, perhaps the best way to give you an idea of what one might have been like is if I describe my second job.

From the Langham I moved across the road to the BBC's Schools Radio Department. If you are of a certain age you might remember the programmes they made, such as *Singing Together*, *A Religious Service for Primary Schools* and *Music and Movement*. I became secretary to a producer, John Parry, who was responsible for a series for older teenagers called *Inquiry*. John (and we were on first-name terms, unlike at the SBC) was a burly, affable Liverpudlian in his mid-40s, who had been a university lecturer and had a sideline in English Language textbooks and horror stories. 'In this business,' he said, 'it pays to keep as many irons as possible in the fire.'

The morning began with my arriving at the office around 9.30 am. First I opened the post, clipping the envelopes to the backs of the letters, sorting them in order of priority and placing the pile on his desk; for this you had to be aware of what your boss considered important so some management memos went straight to the bottom. Then I got on with any work of my own left over from the previous day.

John's arrival at about 10.15 am signalled my departure to the Broadcasting House canteen to fetch coffee for us both. By the time I returned, he would be ready to dictate replies to the correspondence and hand back any letters he thought I could answer myself: actors looking for work perhaps, or trainee teachers wanting information about our programmes. The rest of the day would consist of typing back my shorthand notes, making phone calls and appointments, typing reports and scripts and getting them duplicated, and filing copies of everything.

Taking shorthand dictation occupied between a fifth and a quarter of the working day. Depending on how you and your boss got on, these sessions might be strictly functional or the morning's entertainment. John would explain before he began dictating what he was going to say in each letter and why, which was helpful when I came to decipher my terrible shorthand notes but more importantly gave me an opportunity to ask him questions about the business. Better still, on less busy days these sessions turned into quasi-tutorials about politics, literature and history. For example, John, hearing one morning that I knew nothing about Bertoldt Brecht, took the phone off the hook, closed the office door and gave me a 40-minute lecture on twentieth-century German theatre. In return I was, he said, his 'sounding board', someone at whom he could throw ideas and compare options. Actually, it was one of the most enjoyable but least recognised parts of any secretary's job, which barely received any public attention, perhaps because the men wanted their decisions to look as if they had been made by them alone.

Writing shorthand, sitting with pad on knee in the boss's office, was much less troublesome than it had been at college. Knowing the context of what was being dictated was a big help and the business vocabulary of most bosses didn't stretch beyond a few hundred words.

Sarah Oram
Computing, London

'Although I learned how to take dictation, no boss I ever came across had been taught to dictate. In most cases they would write out what they wanted to say first and then read it to me. So I would say, "Look, give me the piece of paper". And after most bosses got to know me they'd just ask me to send a letter to So-and-So saying whatever, I'd write it and he'd just check it.'

Verity Martin
Hospital, Bristol

'I used to have to take minutes for the Renal Transplant Steering Group. Shorthand was fine until it came to trying to write the very long name of a new drug and then remembering what the devil it was when transcribing.'

Olwen Hanson
Engineering, Yorkshire

'The language used in the 1970s was more formal, even archaic in some cases. I remember automatically changing the dictated "We are in receipt of your esteemed communication of 28th ultimo" to simply say, "Thank you for your letter dated 28th October". Punctuation was important, with the use of full-stops after all abbreviations, commas scattered throughout letters and single or double quotation marks as appropriate. Highlighting words meant either switching the ribbon selector to red or changing the whole ribbon. Ragged right-hand margins meant that secretaries had to know the correct way to hyphenate words, as well as having the ability to estimate whether three pages of shorthand notes would fit onto one page of typing. How often these days do we receive auto-printed letters where page two is simply "Yours faithfully" and the sender's signature?'

Gillian Summers
Import/export, London

'The boss came in on the Brighton Belle wearing a top hat, black suit and carried an umbrella. I had to start at 9.00 and worked till 5.00, but my boss didn't get in till 10.00 am. He was very grumpy and stuck to a strict routine. I dreaded the sound of the old lift opening with a clang as he shouted "Gillian, Post!" down the hall. I had to have all his letters ready, opened, each with an envelope pinned to the back and any files related to the sender attached underneath.

'After about half an hour I heard his voice again, "Dictation!" This was my cue to go in with my shorthand notebook, and take down the replies to the earlier letters. He was very pedantic and would state every comma and full stop and how many carbon copies I had to make and who they were for.

'After dictation we had a coffee break when all the secretaries and the girls from accounts and the typing pool would take turns to make the coffee, and then we would take them back to our desks and begin typing.

'Sometimes I would get a word wrong or, thinking that he had used the wrong word, change it for a better one. A big mistake. When I put the typed letters on his desk he would never say a word or even look up, but the next thing I would hear was another bellow from his office: "Wrong!" I would creep back, and he would fling the "wrong" letter, scribbled all over with black pen, back at me to type all over again.'

The coffee break was a welcome interruption to the morning's work. If there was a staff room-cum-kitchenette with a kettle, fridge and crockery, it was a chance for the 'secretarial mafia' to gather and share news, as well as seek refreshment. It was also an opportunity for PAs to call in and inform everyone of imminent changes, who was going to look after a new member of staff and where she would be working. Secretaries could fix appointments for their bosses without having to trouble the men — who were always impressed with the arrangements even if they didn't realise how they had been made. Best of all, it was a chance to chat.

It's easy to underestimate how useful this network was in oiling the administrative wheels, smoothing out niggles and misunderstandings. It was also great therapy. Problem boyfriends, awkward flatmates and irritating relatives were picked over; advice was liberally handed out which, if ignored, provided more matter for debate. Above all, friendships were formed, many of which lasted long after the people concerned ceased working together.

Mary L Cryns
San Francisco

'It [the building] was mostly built in the earlier 1900s with the beautiful lobby and old creaky elevators which scared me. We didn't have a "real" break room or a kitchen, just a storage room that all of us would pile into during break time. We'd joke around and laugh and carry on about anything and everything. Oh, and we talked incessantly about the brand new *Star Wars* movie which came out in 1977 and how we'd all seen it several times, standing in the long lines. Or the latest records which came out, or what concerts we went to. One secretary was in love with Jackson Browne (she ended up marrying her attorney, who was one of the younger ones!). All in that crazy little storage room.'

The boss needed his morning coffee too, which was usually provided by his secretary. If she didn't make it herself she might collect it from a serviced tea trolley (the rumble of its distant approach was always eagerly anticipated), a vending machine or cafe nearby.

Amanda Lunt
BBC Radio, London

'In BBC radio studios, you fetched drinks for the whole team from the canteen upstairs. Recording tape spools proved invaluable for this, as you could fit six plastic mugs inside the gaps in the metal spool and carry them up and down stairs, in lifts and along corridors without (usually) spilling a drop, though the somewhat aggressive fire doors in Broadcasting House could set a trap for the unwary.

'One producer engaged Sir John Gielgud. I was asked to bring a cup of coffee into the studio and shook hands with the great man. As I retreated to the door I heard him say (in the kind of *faux pas* for which he was notorious) "It seems a shame that so many otherwise attractive girls just don't know how to do themselves justice." This could only have been aimed at me, who at the time was wearing, for comfort and practicality, a checked shirt and corduroys. As I returned to the control cubicle I was greeted by the guffaws of the two male studio managers.'

*****

Copy typing, from handwritten drafts or standard forms, could form part of a general secretary's job or it might be the responsibility of a dedicated typist occupying the next step down the pyramid. During the 70s they became superseded by audio typists, who used headphones to listen to a section of dictation recorded on cassette tapes, typed it back and then listened to another bit, using a foot pedal to stop and start the recording. The secret challenge of audio typing was to type so fast that you didn't need to keep pressing the pedal.

Mary L Cryns
Law firm, San Francisco.

'I'd go into the attorney's office and grab a giant stack of files with a tape on top and bring it back to my desk. Then I'd listen to the tape with a headset and foot pedal and do whatever he said, like he'd say, "Type a letter to so-and-so," So I'd have to get the letterhead and carbon paper ready and stick it into my typewriter. The attorney would instruct me what to do on the tape — like call to set up a deposition at a certain number and file a declaration of readiness to proceed. All the instructions were on the tape.

'As a legal secretary, I wasn't that bored. Although one time I was working on a tape for my attorney and he actually put music on the tape for me to listen to while I typed up envelopes. He said that it was music his daughters liked, and they were just a little younger than me. So there I was sitting there, typing away and singing, "I write the songs that make the whole world sing..." at the top of my lungs, not realizing that I was singing loudly because I had the head set in my ears. Apparently, the main partner walked by my desk with a client who remarked, "My, this is a happy office!" I was oblivious, singing away until one of the secretaries ran up to me and tapped me and said I was singing so loud! We all got a good laugh out of that, and talked about it for ages.'

I was never keen on audio work. Wearing headphones under my chin made me feel like I had a beard. Then the connecting cable would catch on the edge of the desk and yank my ears, or I would accidentally kick the pedal into a dark corner under the desk and have to grovel about on the floor to retrieve it. I was never as proficient as the woman who told me she could listen to a Dictaphone and read a book at the same time.

Besides, there were other pitfalls. You could easily put the cassette in the wrong way up, lose your place in the recording by accidentally spooling on, or even erase the whole thing by mistake. Ooops. Then there was the boss who, at the end of a lengthy piece of dictation with a single copy, would add thoughtfully, 'and two extra copies, please', so you had to type it another two copies over again. Then there were times when it was hard to hear what was being said, either because the quality of the tape had deteriorated with repeated use, or because of the circumstances of the recording. One contributor remembered her boss used to record his dictation in German railway stations, so it was obliterated by platform announcements and the sound of trains passing.

Reaching the foot of the pyramid brings us to a place very far from the hushed, wood-panelled walls of a PA's office: to the noisiest room in the building, possibly another building altogether. Welcome to 'The Pool'.

Typing pools were located in out of the way areas because the racket from multiple typewriters was like being in a barrage on the Western Front. And it went on all day. Pools were one of those splendid inventions from the 1920s' scientific management movement, designed to streamline document production in the same way that conveyor belts had in factories. Companies with copious amounts of paperwork stocked a room with typists, gave them all the routine typing: invoices, sales proposals, standard letters, marketing circulars and so on, and put them under the supervision of an older woman, probably a former secretary, whose job it was to ensure its output was accurate and timely.

The pool loomed as a kind of infernal pit to the middling sort of secretary, somewhere she might be sent if her work didn't come up to scratch; which was an unfair (if effective) way of keeping her on her toes. In fact, plenty of secretaries did their time in pools and some preferred audio or copy work to struggling with shorthand. Pools varied in size, they might have only four or five typists or as many as 30 or 40, depending on the size of the company. They were mini-societies on their own, isolated from the rest of the company, with their own internal hierarchy and customs which it was unwise to flout. The typists there were usually more down to earth and assertive than their sisters in the upper ranks — as one civil servant told me, 'I remember a senior civil servant patronisingly advised a pool typist that there were three 'l's in 'parallel'; "Aye," she replied, "and three 'f's in f*** off."

Margaret Knowles
Various, Wolverhampton

'Just because you were a copy typist did not mean you were dim. Certain things had to be typed. There were all ages in a typing pool, not just young girls. I worked in a typing pool and got on rather well. The work wasn't boring because you never had the same job twice, you were working for different departments who brought their work up there to be typed.'

Hazel Rees
Electrical engineering company, Bedford

'I felt a bit like a battery hen. The typing was done from recorded tapes which came from various employees, so you never knew who you were typing for. You sat in lines, probably about 20 to 25 typists, all with your earphones in as you clattered away. I don't really like working with lots of other women, the atmosphere was a bit catty, and as I was only 16 it could sometimes feel a bit intimidating.'

Alison Chubb
Domestic appliances manufacturer, London

'All the desks faced the same way like at school, and an elderly dragon sat on a stage in front of us. Her only job seemed to be watching us closely all day long. She gave us all a different five-minute slot to go to the toilet in the morning and afternoon. We weren't supposed to go at any other time, and at times of a heavy period I used to worry whether my tampon would last out!'

Christine Allsop
Motoring group, Chesterfield

'The work was distributed equally in the morning, sometimes we had it all done by 10.30 or 11.00 am. We would then play warships and similar games for the rest of the day. We would go to the pub at lunch time and if it was someone's birthday everyone would get drunk.'

*****

An important part of the secretary's job was to be in the office to answer telephone calls, usually referred to as 'manning the phone'. This was an expression I always found amusing, why not 'womanning' it? Large organisations like the BBC had switchboards to route calls through to the appropriate extension, so in Schools Radio when I answered the phone I had to decide whether to deal with it myself, put it through to John or, if he was out, take a message or pass the caller on to someone else. When your boss was away from the office, or in a meeting that couldn't be interrupted, you had to hope there wasn't a crisis call.

Heather Pippins
Builders' merchants, Yeovil.

> It was a big company, and it was the main board that was meeting that day. You couldn't just walk in and interrupt them.
> 'One of the branch managers phoned up and said, "I've got to talk to your boss urgently, Heather."
> I said, "He's in a board meeting."
> "No, I've really got to talk to him urgently, you've got to go in there."
> I said, "Why?"
> "Well, when we got in this morning half the yard had disappeared, and half the office building with it!"
> I said, "Are you kidding me?"
> He said, "No, I'm not kidding you, Heather. I'm sitting in the showroom, but even a piece of that's fallen down the hole.'

The buildings had been constructed on the site of a disused quarry and had collapsed overnight (remember this was a firm of builders' merchants). Heather dutifully waited until she took the tray of morning coffee into the meeting, when she slipped a note to her boss. To great relief he came out to deal with the emergency.

Sometimes the etiquette surrounding meetings defied commonsense.

Kathryn Vaughan
BBC administration, London

'I saw some guy going into a meeting, and asked him if he would hand a document to my boss who was already in there. It caused a furore. It turned out he was Head of Something or Other and should never have been asked to perform such a menial task. I thought I'd been using my initiative.'

*****

Midday. Time for a lunch break. What that involved depended what the employer offered: staff canteen or do it yourself. Canteens, which Jilly Cooper, in her book *How to Survive from Nine to Five,* said reminded her of school dinners, were only provided by large companies.

Amanda Lunt
BBC Radio, London

'The main BBC buildings all had subsidised canteens, mostly very well run and, even if the menus could be a bit predictable, the quality was good and the prices reasonable. They were the ideal way for single people to get their main meal of the day, as well as a place to socialise. There were also tea and snack bars selling salads and sandwiches, and of course the bars and buffets selling light meals run by the BBC Club.'

Catherine Preston
BBC Television, London

'At Television Centre the *Doctor Who* monsters had to cope with the restrictions of their costumes. They put me off my lunch! Cybermen could take their helmets off, but the eight-legged creepy monsters had difficulty eating while not knocking over everything nearby. It was always funny to watch them.'

Lorraine Oliver
Guinness Brewery, Park Royal, London

'The brewery gave us free three-course lunches and included a half pint of beer or lager.'

Jilly, I don't remember that being offered at my school. At the BBC's Television Centre, senior managers entertained their visitors in a separate silver service restaurant on the floor above the canteen, in complete safety of course because Daleks couldn't climb the stairs. It was common practice for companies to separate their dining facilities in this way.

Christine Allsop
Engineering company, Chesterfield

'The works canteen was segregated into four sections: shop floor, office works, managers, directors. All the managers went to the pub every lunch time drinking, or they went to the directors' dining room for lunch where there was a bar. In my opinion the secretarial and clerical staff, along with middle managers, did all the work there.

'I was once told that I had to go for lunch with my boss's boss and his PA. The four of us went to a local restaurant. I did not want to go because I was scared of someone seeing me and what they would think. I was a married woman, and I lived in a small village where everyone knew each other. This restaurant was very near where I lived, and I wondered what anyone would think of me dining out with two men, it was not the done thing at the time. But I had no choice. I asked the PA what I should order off the menu and she said the dearest thing. I thought about it and did just that. They deserved it and I hoped it would mean they would not ask me again.'

Jane Green
Manufacturing plant, Slough

'Everyone left their desks at the same time for lunch. No one ate a picnic at their desks in those days, that was unheard of. There were two canteens downstairs: one for the shop floor workers, and one for the office staff and management. Our canteen had nicer chairs and better crockery and cutlery.'

Where there was no canteen, employees headed to a local cafe or sandwich bar for supplies. This was long before the days of flat whites, blueberry muffins and tortilla wraps.

Mary L Cryns
Law firm, San Francisco

'I would get black coffee for my attorney in the morning, and every day he sent me out to a sandwich place down the street to pick up a plain cheese sandwich on white bread, a milk and a Milky Way candy bar. This guy ate that EVERY SINGLE DAY! He also gave me enough extra money to buy myself a sandwich too, which was cool. It didn't seem abnormal at all for this at the time, and I didn't mind especially because I got a free sandwich out of the deal.

'So I'd bring my sandwich back to work, deliver his cheese sandwich and usually just ate either at my desk or I'd walk outside and eat down at Union Square in San Francisco. Sometimes I'd go to the local Discount Records store which was close to my work, and I remember writing my very first check there after getting a checking account. I was so excited about that. Occasionally, I'd go out to lunch with other secretaries, but only occasionally.'

In the UK, firms offered Luncheon Vouchers (LVs), a nationwide government scheme from the days of post-war rationing subsidising the cost of meals in cafes and sandwich bars.

Sarah Oram
Computing, London

'You used to go to sandwich bars. Er, you did go to the pub, but that's probably another story ... Anyway, the sandwich bars. There was a chain called "Queens", and they were everywhere. I suppose the nearest modern equivalent is probably something like Subway. It was like a conveyor belt. You went in and you'd name your combination. I liked cream cheese with ham, or cheese and pickle with cucumber. "White or brown bread?" And this would be made up in front of you, with somebody buttering the bread, the next person putting one filling on, someone else the next, and when you got to the end it would be wrapped and you paid up.'

Deirdre Hyde
Book publishers, London

'I joined the other secretaries in a communal kitchen, all of us with our plastic boxes and sandwiches. Some knitted, some read books, conversation was general, no politics or religion, definitely no sex or love lives. Sandwiches were white, sliced bread. Grated cheese with flaccid tomatoes. Sliced ham, corned beef. And they came in a paper bag. No baguettes that I recall.

'Then the sandwich shops began to get more adventurous with plastic tubs of coleslaw, and egg mayonnaise. Maybe even prawns. And soup in polystyrene foam cups: chicken or tomato. I seem to remember them as mostly Italian — the shops not the sandwiches. Usually eaten at one's desk, so with four or five in one room it was quite sociable. In the summer we might go out together and sit in the park.'

Canny secretaries hoarded their LVs and either swapped them for bread and cakes to eat at home or waited until the end of the week to enjoy a slap-up, three-course meal.

The most unusual lunch arrangement I came across was at a publishing company, where I went to work after the BBC. This was William Kimber and Co, where I was one of only seven employees, so it was a big change from being one of many thousands at the Corporation. I was secretary to the boss, William Kimber, a brilliant publisher and an erudite but neurotic individual.

To avoid having to give out LVs he claimed that the firm had a canteen. In practice, this meant that as soon as he had set off for his lunch at the Garrick Club, the sole (female) editor would dash into the 'kitchen', an unventilated cupboard with a two-ring electric hob, to cook lunch for herself, the two accounts girls and me. Her specialities were Tuna Fish Pie (tinned tuna in cheese sauce poured over boiled potatoes), Potatoes, Hard-boiled Eggs and Watercress in Vinaigrette sauce and her signature dish, Fried Spam with Lentils. We ate these delicacies standing up in the kitchen so the offices wouldn't smell of food. She was a good cook and the meals were surprisingly delicious, we contributed around 20p each to the cost of ingredients and took turns to wash the dishes afterwards, averting our gaze from the liberal distribution of mouse droppings on the carpet.

*****

Lunch over, it was time to get back to work and tackle the less usual duties of the job. At the BBC in my radio production days, this meant tracking the progress of every programme from commission to broadcast on a large handwritten chart pinned to the noticeboard behind my desk. Scripts went through two or three drafts before the final version was agreed, each of which had to be typed and copied. I also booked studios, actors, musicians and writers, for which multiple copies of forms had to be sent (everything at the BBC came with at least three copies, apart from the tea and the salary). I transcribed tape-recorded interviews so that John could choose the sections to use in the programmes, ordered records from the BBC's extensive Gramophone Library for the music breaks (plus a few for personal listening, of course) and listed any used in a programme for payment to the PRS (Performing Rights Society); and wrote the brief details of each programme for the *Radio Times*. Before transmission, I sent a copy of the script with a form known as a 'P as B' (Programme As Broadcast). This listed all the details of the programme, writer, producer, music used and so on, but, strangely enough, not the secretary. There was a space at the bottom of the form to warn the on-air presenter if the programme had a false ending or a loud explosion in the last 20 seconds so he wasn't too discombobulated to make the next announcement. At the end of the day, around 5.00 pm, a BBC postman collected the outgoing post from a tray inside our office door and our own copies were stowed away in arch-lever files.

In this job I was at times required to work at weekends. The BBC ran 24/7, so it wasn't a problem. John particularly liked to record his programmes then — I think it had something to do with his mother-in-law's habit of making extended visits to his home. Recording sessions began with a rehearsal, during which I sat in the control cubicle with my thumb on a stopwatch and a biro in the other hand, writing down the time at appropriate moments in the script so that, if it looked like the programme might overrun, we could cut the script before recording. Editing after recording was time consuming. In those days of reel-to-reel machines it was done by a junior engineer chopping through the tape with a razor blade, removing the unwanted section of tape and joining the cut ends together with sticky tape. Fortunately, John was very efficient at making sure the script was about the right length before we went into the studio, so there was seldom any editing to done.

Apart from fetching cups of tea for the cast and crew, timing the programme was my only duty in the studio so it was a little galling that John also used his own stopwatch. I think he started doing it after I confidently announced a programme was 18 minutes and 99 seconds long. Nevertheless, it was always interesting to see the programmes come together. I was in constant awe at the skill of the studio managers, minor radio celebrities like journalist John Tusa and actor Norman Shelley and writers like Jim Crace, Willy Russell and David Edgar, all of whom worked on the series.

Others had interesting and unusual extra duties too.

Sue MacCulloch
Northwick Park Hospital, Middlesex

'As a consultant's secretary, I had contact with patients because they would be phoning and coming to clinics. They wanted to talk to somebody, not necessarily that we could sort something out, but they just needed to talk, and there was a lot more time to listen to and speak to them. I took a course in counselling which was helpful, although only on an amateur basis. I paid for it myself. Even in those days they didn't put money into things they didn't have to.'

Jan Jones
Co-Operative Wholesale Society, Manchester

'I would co-ordinate promotions and competitions. I remember having to open the competition entries one year. They came by the sackful, and some of the answers to the tie-breakers were hysterically funny because they were so bad. Also, a lot of the envelopes weren't franked, so after some careful steaming I ended up with enough stamps to last me a couple of years.'

Heather Pippins
Johnson & Johnson, Slough

'I hadn't realised that in the Marketing Department you would have to deal with customers' complaints. People would write in saying they'd bought a tin of talcum powder and the lid had come off, and they would post it to you like that. I was showered with talcum powder several times. After a while I did get a bit fed up with it.'

Valerie Docker
BBC administration, London

'There were many BBC canteens dotted around the country, and I worked for one of the administrators in an office near Broadcasting House. It had lots of mahogany, and was very quiet. The head of the department was the Head of Catering, so the other members of staff jokingly called him "Top Cat". They thought this was very funny, and mentioned it several times.

'I worked for the woman who was about third down the list. My job was to answer her phone — if she got a call, of which weren't many — and she got about three letters a day which I had to record in a ledger, type a response, put that in the mail and record that in the ledger too. So we had a good handle on all that correspondence.'

Tanya Bruce Lockhart
London Weekend Television, Central London

'When I first arrived, there were a lot of desperate men running around with piles of unopened envelopes. They were letters from people who wanted to work at LWT, and I was told to sort them into people who were probables, who had to have previous experience in television, and people who were possibles, the ones who wrote good letters. It was all left to me which, for somebody aged just 21, was quite a responsibility. And when I wasn't doing that I was making the tea. That didn't matter, I was very happy to be one of the team. To be in at the beginning of something is terrific. I thought the world was my oyster.'

Kathryn Vaughan
The College of Psychic Studies, London

'The CPS was founded in the late nineteenth century: I'll just say that it was quite an old-fashioned organisation. It had its roots in the interest in psychic matters during the late 19th century and developed alongside the Society for Psychical Research. The SPR was interested in the science behind apparently illogical happenings, while the College was more concerned with the possibility of communication with the dead and therefore the possibility of a life after death. With the exception of a growing group of young members through the 60s, the membership was predominantly middle-aged and middle-to-upper class.

'I was the PA to the President, who worked part-time. My role was to manage his personal involvement with the College, and also I had to type up whichever book he was working on at the time. He had terribly small, crabby writing, so was delighted by the fact that I could usually read it.

'Because the College premises were quite small, the admin staff and [psychic] mediums did come across each other occasionally and generally we got on well. Of course the mediums had private rooms for their consultations, but sometimes there might be problems, a medium might have a meltdown, so we would calm them down with a cup of tea and a chat.'

Doreen Ashpole
Not disclosed, Cambridge

'I took on whatever was needing doing. Some were really strange, like getting a visitor's suitcase mended, taking the excess cardboard to the tip, overseeing the cleaning contracts, arranging committee meetings, diary dates, international travel arrangements, pricing handouts and so much more.

'I stapled up the boss's diary if I knew his wife wanted to go on holiday. When I was being chased for replies, I wrote the letters or references myself for him to sign. If I hadn't they would still be in his in-tray today.'

Very occasionally work took us outside the office. At the end of the 70s I worked in BBC television drama, and for a couple of days joined the team filming a mini-series called *The Lost Boys* on location in Kensington Gardens.

My job was to prevent members of the public from wandering into shot. On Day One, in glorious sunshine, I took up my position near the Albert Memorial and watched small children in Edwardian costumes bowling hoops up and down Lancaster Walk while the camera rolled. A group of German tourists, whom I had detained for a few minutes, observed this scene with great amusement and asked was this how English children normally entertained themselves? I'm sorry to say that I took my new-found responsibilities very seriously and failed to see the joke.

On Day Two the temperature plummeted by 20 degrees. Drizzle thickened into steady rain, completely dissolving the glamour of show-biz. Ian Holm, the actor playing the leading role of J.M. Barrie, swathed in a huge greatcoat and scarf, shivered unhappily. My boss furtively slipped me a fiver and despatched me to Bayswater to purchase a half-bottle of whiskey. On my return Mr Holm was quickly revived, and shortly afterwards a queue formed at the catering truck for Uncle Louis' Special Coffee.

Deirdre Hyde
Book publishers, London

'I took part in the planning of, and attendance at, book launches attended by journalists who would hopefully give the book a good write-up, booksellers who might put in a good order, and (any useful) friends and contacts of the author.

'One of my first such events was held one morning at Australia House when I had only been in the job for a few weeks. I was terribly nervous. I didn't really have a role once it was under way. No one came and talked to me, and I had no idea of how to introduce myself to anyone. Or indeed what to say if I did. Positioned in a corner beside a massive potted plant, I did, however, take a drink every time one of the waiters walked by with a loaded tray. My boss found me eventually and realised I was completely plastered. Fifty years on I still go hot and cold remembering the ignominy of being helped down the steps and bundled into a cab back to Fleet Street, where I promptly threw up on the pavement outside the *Daily Express* offices. Amazingly, I kept my job.'

Andrea Sarner
Film company, London

'Sometimes I was invited to watch new films in the little viewing cinema. I took two writers to see the movie of M*A*S*H, as they had been commissioned to write the TV series. When this amazing film finished, they just looked at each other and said "Shit!"! Of course they wrote a wonderful series which, like the film, was a huge hit.

'In the same little cinema I sat next to Lord Snowdon to watch *A Clockwork Orange*. the director Stanley Kubrick sat at the back. To start the screening, he picked up the intercom to the projectionist and said, "Roll 'em!". Then he put down the phone and said, "I've always wanted to say that!'

*****

However, most days were spent in the office and most days were busy; but there were always those when the boss had gone out, work had been done and there was little left in the in-tray. Long afternoons dragged on, the hands on the clock fell asleep and the heap of paper in the filing tray sulked reproachfully. It's a funny thing, but once momentum at work was lost it was difficult to find it again, and it was surprising how resentful I felt if someone appeared with work half an hour before home time.

My favourite distraction was to read the Post Office Guide, which was full of information about things like how you couldn't send chewing gum to the USSR or import sausages from Australia. After that, I could usually find another underemployed secretary to grumble with about how we were paid to do so little and couldn't we do more. After all, a grumble shared is a grumble magnified.

Amanda Lunt
BBC Radio, London

'Boredom did strike from time to time, usually when left alone in the office to type up something fairly dreary. One job largely entailed filing away telexes from foreign broadcasting organisations. Fortunately, in this case the senior secretary and I shared the same sense of humour and spent part of one quiet afternoon casting the other members of the production team as characters in *Winnie-the-Pooh*.'

Carol Brinson
Temp, London

'One place didn't seem to really need me — I spent a lot of time playing Pontoon for paper clips with a colleague.'

Debbie Maya
BBC World Service, London

'My job was typing letters written out in rough by the engineers and answering the telephone to customers who wanted to know how they could pick up the World Service abroad and on what frequencies. I had to send telexes. Boring? Oh yeah. It was boring, boring, boring. I used to go off and have a fag. Also, I started an affair with one of the Russian section. Anything to stave off the boredom.'

*****

The end of the working day was signalled by a sudden rush to get all the letters and parcels ready for the last post. This was vital because even a day's delay might mean missing a deadline or losing a contract. The boss would be given a folder inside which the newly typed letters were interleaved with sheets of blotting paper. He would check and sign each one, unless he had changed his mind or found too many mistakes for it to be sent out (also known as 'I've changed my mind about this one'). If at this critical time he was nowhere to be found, his secretary would sign the letters in her own name on his behalf: others, of whom we shall not speak, became adept at forging signatures.

Gillian Summers
Import/Export company, Central London

'The last job of the day was to collect all the signed letters from the bosses' office desks and take them to the post-room, where the top page was folded neatly so that when the recipient opened the letter the address would show at the front. We put all of them through the franking machine, turning a handle like an old-fashioned mangle. Then all the carbon copies had to be filed in great metal filing cabinets before we could go home.'

Did anyone skive off early? There were afternoons when work had been completed and going home a few minutes, maybe half an hour, earlier seemed sensible. But there was always the dratted telephone and, in the days before answerphones, you didn't want to miss an important call. At one place a senior secretary, a typical BBB (BusyBody-with-Bun), would appear in my office at 5.25 pm to make sure I was still poised by the phone, womanning it. I knew what she was up to, and she knew I knew, so a strange and meaningless dialogue would ensure about the characteristics of spider plants or the efficiency of pencil sharpeners, until it was 5.30 pm when I could stand up and say, 'Goodness me, is that the time?'

Phyllida Scrivens
B.P. Chemicals, London

'Sneaking out before 5.00 pm was quite an acceptable practice especially if you could claim that the trains had problems and you had to get home. In the winter we constantly monitored the temperature, once demanding to be sent home as it had gone below the acceptable minimum. I cannot imagine life in a major corporate is that relaxed nowadays.'

Verity Lamb
Not disclosed, Glasgow

'I knew of one girl who shared an office with another, older woman. The job was very dull, so when her companion wasn't in the room she would get up on a chair and wind the hands on the clock forward by half an hour so she could leave early. I don't think anybody ever noticed.'

On the other hand, one secretary at a television company hung around until 2.00 am once because John and Yoko Lennon were expected to pop in. Alas, they never showed and she wasn't paid overtime either. But most secretaries headed home, to the pub, or to a company social club.

Terri Kaye
Beechams Pharmaceuticals, London

'Eventually the other people I worked with said, "Are you coming to the Club on Friday?" I said, "Club? What club?"'

'It was a nice evening. We had cheaper drinks, because unknown to me Beecham's owned drinks companies like

Campari, with peanuts and crisps to keep us going and there was a lot of chin-wagging going on. If we stayed to the end, around 9.30 pm we'd say, "Right, where are we going for supper?" The only places that were still open then were for curries and we had our favourite curry house. I hate to say it but we used to drive there even though we'd been drinking. It's embarrassing now to think we did.'

Amanda Lunt
BBC Radio, London

'The weekly routine was much enhanced by membership of the BBC Club, an independently financed entity run largely on the profits of the bars and buffets in BBC premises around the country. It boasted a vast array of sections devoted to all kinds of sport and other interests from archery to wine-making, providing a chance to socialise and acquire skills in safe surroundings, and find out what went on in other departments and what career opportunities might be on offer — what is nowadays known as networking.'

Elaine Day
BBC Television, London

'I was definitely burning the candle at both ends. I joined the BBC Club's Studio Amateur Dramatic Group and got a lead part on my first audition. I can remember going to SADG rehearsals many nights in a row, and having a meal in the BH canteen first, it was such fun.'

Sometimes a secretary might be asked to attend an evening function.

Andrea Sarner
Film company, London

'Working for the television department of a major film company I went to film premieres. Most of the celebrities were charming and polite, including Michael Caine and Roger Moore to whom I served champagne at a premiere, wearing a low-cut evening dress and a sash (me, not them). The press were more interested in Twiggy. I had previously seen Michael Caine when he came into the offices, because the secretary of the publicity manager rang me and said, "Wait in the lobby, he's about to arrive", so I sat in a chair and pretended I was waiting for somebody else.'

Gloria Miles
Solicitors, City of London

'All the men who worked in the City at this time wore pin-striped trousers, waistcoats with watch chains and black jackets. They wore bowler hats outside of the office and carried umbrellas. Mr John Welch was a very nice man to work for, and he was also the Clerk of the Worshipful Company of Furniture Makers. I had the minutes to type up from meetings he went to, and when there was an evening function I was given an amount of money to buy or hire an evening dress and get my hair done to meet the guests at the Mansion House and make sure they were all taken to their appropriate tables for their meals. These were evening events and I was always taken home afterwards so there was no problem with being about being late; and the next day did not have to be at work until 10.00 am instead of 9.00 am.'

Eventually the working day came to an end. The lights in the building were turned off, the phones fell silent and the typewriters were tucked up snugly in their covers at last. It was all over, at least until the next working day.

Chapter 3 : Temperatures, typewriters and subversive trousers

Every now and again something reminds me of the 70s. Photos do: of guys in wallpaper-patterned shirts underneath knitted tank tops, girls in knee-high suede boots and perilously short skirts. A few seconds of what was then called a 'record,' a vinyl disc by Slade or Bowie or Pete Atkin singing Clive James's lyrics, sends me back to evenings in a bedsit sipping whiskey and wondering where were all the crazy parties that were supposed to be happening. But as I can't play those tracks to you here I will try to evoke that decade as it was experienced by secretaries.

What do others remember?

- 'Secretaries with headsets in their ears. The office always smelled like coffee. Shelves and shelves of paper and forms.'

- 'The smell of envelope glue – mmm! The drumming sound of a room full of people typing. Two-tier wire baskets that were hell to assemble. Dried-up pot plants.'

- 'GripFix, a glue with its distinct smell of almonds. It came in a small pot with a little integral spreader which fitted into the plastic lid.'

- 'The constant whistling from one colleague, the blue haze of pipe-smoke permeating from another; mishearing the boss's wife when she rang through with her weekly shopping list, resulting in his taking home kippers instead of peppers (which I'd never heard of) and, when I handed in my notice, the silence when my boss refused to speak to me for two weeks.'

- 'The smell of brown lino along the floors of all the corridors; except the top one where the bosses' offices were; that had rugs on top.'

- 'Heels clicking on the wooden floors when one of the secretaries was called to take dictation. If we couldn't spell something she would shout out to us, "two Ns, one L" or whatever the word was.'

- 'A very old building in the centre of Huddersfield. Our offices were on the first floor and the toilets were very dark and dingy, but at least they weren't cold.'

- 'The smells of the city: bus exhaust, dirty water, hot dogs, vagrants.'

Let's take a look at three particular aspects of this world: office buildings, from the antique to the super-modern, equipment — typewriters, telephones and duplicators — and clothes, where we will discover a controversy that today seems unbelievable.

First, office buildings. These ranged from decrepit, patched-up old houses with wonky floors and solid doors to shiny new tower blocks that rose like glass teeth above the city streets. In the decades leading up to the 70s, UK cities had been struggling to recover from wartime damage and neglect, and to meet the growing demand for office space, old houses were quickly and cheaply converted.

I've already mentioned that the Langham, where I first worked, had originally been a grand hotel. Unusually for a junior shorthand/typist, there I had an office to myself. It was furnished with a plain wooden desk and chair, beside which stood a table with a telephone, and a small wooden chest with drawers for each different kind of stationery: letterhead, copy, plain and carbon sheets of paper and envelopes of all sizes. Around the walls were shelves of boxes full of publications. The window, facing north, gave a stunning view across the roofs of Portland Place to the tips of the trees in Regent's Park. I was Rapunzel at the top of her tower.

The Langham had been bombed during the war, and so badly damaged that there were still cracks in the walls wide enough to stuff newspaper into on cold days. Like other old buildings, the adaptations were rough and ready and the heating often erratic or non-existent. In another building, an old house in Kensington, the secretary had to light an open coal fire each winter morning.

Georgian town houses, of which there were many in London, had steep, narrow stairs to the upper floors, originally designed for the sole use of maidservants. Now secretaries wearing high-heels had to struggle up and down them balancing tea trays, hoping they didn't slip and fall. At least on the lower floors staircases built for the gentry offered a softer landing.

Sarah Oram
Computing, London

'I remember how, in the 70s, run-down the buildings were, and how generally undecorated, ungentrified everything was. If you think of some of those gorgeous Kensington properties that have the pillars by the front doors, in those days they were multi-occupancy houses with cracked plastering, cracked paintwork, like you see in black and white films. There's no possible comparison between what London is like now and what it was then.

'In Belgrave Square I worked in an office converted from a most lovely building with a wonderful staircase that swept up. It was carpeted, the steps were very shallow and quite wide. I fell down it once. I don't know what happened, I was sober, I must have just caught my foot at the top. It was like rolling down a slope, down to the bottom. I wasn't hurt. I must have made a habit of it, because I did it somewhere else as well, and that was slightly more dramatic. Thank God there was somebody there who grabbed me as I fell because it was a stone staircase. I've still got dents on my shins from it.'

The publishing company of William Kimber occupied a similar eighteenth-century mansion in Westminster. This too had an elegant sweeping staircase, but once you reached the top of it you were confronted by a huge, ugly chipboard partition into which a doorway had been cut. Stepping through that brought you into what had once been a ballroom, a huge room crudely divided by more chipboard. My desk was just inside the doorway: at the opposite end, in front of a huge window overlooking St James's Park, sat two accounts girls. The only reminder of the ballroom's former elegance was its beautiful painted ceiling. I often wondered whether the ghosts of former occupants haunted the attics, waiting until nightfall to come down and gavotte round the filing cabinets.

Anne Ballard
Temporary secretary, London

'I had a huge number of different jobs once I moved to London. I worked in all sorts of offices, some very pleasant and some grim.

'There was a beautiful Georgian house on a London square, with antique furniture and ornaments. And a Dickensian tenement in the City with a Dickensian boss. A slight exaggeration: the office was certainly Dickensian, one of these crumbling tenements in the City with too little lighting and too many stairs. No high stools or quill pens though! The man I worked for was slightly more modern; perhaps stuck in the 1930s. He wore what must have been one of the last bowler hats in London, which was too big for him, and was seldom seen without a filterless cigarette dangling from the lower lip and dripping ash. And his office had dusty old files piled all the way up one wall. Other than that he was quite sweet, but dictated incredibly fast.'

In the 1930s, new factories sprang up on the outskirts of cities. These incorporated purpose-designed offices with corrugated asbestos roofs and single-glazed, metal-framed windows.

Mary Ankrett
Walsall, West Midlands

'There was a two-floor factory of printing presses, ancillary equipment, paper warehouse, artist studio, photographic department, and a two-storey office block, with individual offices for each department: costing, purchasing, accounts, production management and a canteen. No lifts to the second floor in the office block, but a service lift in the printing press areas.

'I worked in the boardroom suite. There were separate offices for the secretary, the MD, the boardroom, a secure filing room and toilet facilities. All the offices in this suite had light oak wooden panelling. I liked my office, which had my desk with an Adler electric typewriter, filing cabinet, an old-fashioned photocopier, a cupboard containing special china for use in the boardroom and a small library of books about the printing industry.

'The décor of the departments was fairly basic as they were separated by wooden panels with windows. Departmental managers had small cubicle offices to keep them apart from the clerks so that they could have private discussions. One could see clerks busy with pens, people on telephones, lots of shelves with folders full of documents. The central heating which had been added after the building was built was not very efficient so one had to make sure of wearing warm clothing in the winter.'

Post-war, a new approach to office building had been demanded. Tower blocks of steel and glass shot up with interiors fitted out in a style known as 'Burolandschaft.' This had (ironically) been developed in Germany from open-plan offices in America, here it was known as 'open-plan' design. The philosophy behind it was to break down existing hierarchical organisational structures and encourage greater team-working by abolishing internal dividing walls. Fewer barriers would lead to better communication and more efficient workflows. Senior managers remained secluded in their cellular offices, but everyone else sat in a wide, open landscape with areas marked out by steel cabinets and Swiss cheese plants. Instead of bare floorboards and linoleum there were fitted carpets in 'cheerful' colours, like orange and turquoise, and the spaces were brightly lit by fluorescent tubes — strip lighting — because anyone working in the centre of the room was too far from the windows to benefit from natural light.

An evangelical zeal about the concept contributed to their general adoption, although perhaps the major attraction was, for the developer, the reduced costs of building without internal structures. Employers were able to pack more people into a building than before and still have enough room for the big mainframe computers which had been difficult to fit into little old buildings.

Open-plan offices were spacious, informal and hugely distracting. Attempts to suppress the level of noise with acoustic ceiling tiles were only ever partially successful. The Managing Director of Penguin Books, surveying his new open-plan domain, admitted that they should never have bought telephones that rang bells[6]. Another complaint was a loss of privacy. Everyone was now able to see what everyone else was up to, especially the managers from behind their glass partitions, but these concerns were brushed aside by claims that it was only employees who felt they could no longer arrive late or doze off after lunch who were unhappy[7]. After all, the building was done now.

My own first experience of working in an open-plan tower block was at a stockbroking firm in the City of London. There was indeed something refreshingly egalitarian about the layout, but it was featureless, just rows of desks and pillars and distant windows. It was also extremely noisy, phones rang almost continually, lively Cockneys chatted all day about boyfriends, husbands, mothers, babies, pop stars and clothes, and outside there was a constant screeching and grinding from the next-door building site.

The job for which I had been hired was copy-typing clients' dividend statements. It was repetitive work, required a lot of attention and the careful use of a ruler and tabulation to make sure the columns of figures lined up correctly. Consequently it was mentally tiring, and sitting at a desk all day without any excuse to get up and walk around was physically exhausting. In fact it was so uncomfortable that when the lunch hour arrived I nearly danced down New Bridge Street.

At the desk next to mine sat a man in his 40s or 50s called George who, unlike any of the other employees, wore the traditional City clerk's pinstripe waistcoat and shirtsleeves. He even put on a bowler hat before he went home. George was a curiosity. It was as if in 1948 he had been told to sit there and had been forgotten about ever since. If he felt out of place amongst those young people he never let it show. Incidentally, he and I were the only two people who arrived each day punctually at 9.30 am.

A few years later, when I went back to work for the BBC, I found myself in another tower block, the (since demolished) East

Tower. This stood behind the iconic 'doughnut' of Television Centre (TC) to which it was linked by a walkway. The tower wasn't open-plan though. Mostly it consisted of traditional, cellular offices, apart from the top floor which was occupied by my boss, myself, and the *Multi-coloured Swap Shop*. However ground-breaking the BBC's programming output was in the 70s, their creative approach didn't extend to office furniture. I was provided with an identical desk, chair and little chest of drawers to those I had used in the Langham ten years before. But at least I had another superb view, this time over Hammersmith, with the sunsets rendered Turneresque by the grime on the windows.

The TC doughnut was an extraordinary building whose circular design made it difficult to navigate, something to do with walking round and round until you came back to where you started. Once, unable to find the canteen, I stopped a woman whom I vaguely recognised, thinking I'd met her before, and asked her the way. With perfect enunciation, she gave me directions. I realised to my horror that I had detained Angela Rippon on her way to read the One O' Clock News and, to my even greater horror, I realised that if, by way of apology for the interruption I said I hadn't recognised her, she might be grossly offended. So I thanked her profusely and promptly set off in the wrong direction.

Let's go back to the problems of tower blocks.

Tanya Bruce Lockhart
London Weekend Television

'We moved to Wembley, where we had the studios we'd taken over from Rediffusion in an office block on the side of the North Circular Road, called Station House, which was grim. It was one of those 20-storey office blocks with sealed windows, you couldn't open them, the air-conditioning was always going wrong so you were either freezing cold or absolutely sweating; and across the road was Harlesden, which was a very impoverished area then, and to the north of us was Wembley Park, and we overlooked this huge, ever-moving North Circular Road.'

Jan Jones
Manchester

'The building I worked in was a skyscraper 13 stories high, very modern for Manchester at that time but not particularly pleasant to work in. There was a definite policy equating the number of windows you had in your office to your standing in the company. The actual office I worked in was probably 80 per cent floor to ceiling glass and faced the sun a lot of the time. If we didn't remember to close the slatted blinds before we left in the evening it became so hot. It was also unpleasant because in those days deodorants weren't worn quite so much and we had one particularly pungent girl in the office.'

What everyone remembers about 70s' offices was the noise. They were full of it: the constant tapping of typewriter keys — you had to stop typing so a colleague could listen to a telephone call — the shrill ringing of telephones and the whirring of dials, steel filing cabinets rattling and squeaking; laughter, shouting, doors slamming, echoing corridors and, if the windows were open, buses, cars, taxis outside with horns, sirens and screeching brakes, even sometimes church bells and birdsong.

One smell pervaded every building: smoke. After a meeting you could walk into a conference room to tidy up and barely be able to see the opposite wall. Smoking in offices was common, one secretary at a hospital puffed her way through several cigarettes a day despite the health warnings on the wall beside her desk. We must all have smelled of fags because pubs, restaurants, trains and buses allowed smoking everywhere except in designated 'No

Smoking' areas. Apart from the risk to health, there was also a real danger of fire.

Sarah Oram
Computing, London

'I used to work with a woman who you'd look at now as a typical "Fag Ash Lil". She always had a fag hanging out of her face, one eye drooping. She smoked filterless Capstan full strength, and when they came in with filters she was extremely annoyed and cut the filters off. When sheets of carbon paper wore out they would be thrown into the waste paper bin, and then on one occasion when she tipped her ashtray into it, there was an almighty "Whoompf!" and flames shot out of it. It died down almost instantaneously, thank God, because it was a grey, metal bin and carbon paper. It was funny though.'

*****

Moving on to equipment, to achieve what a phone or computer and printer can do today, 70s' secretaries had to resort to much lower tech machines. At the start of the decade most in the UK were still using manual typewriters and, like cars and horses, how well they functioned depended on their previous owners. Sometimes a key whacked the ribbon and then declined gracefully like a romantic heroine suffering a fit of the vapours; others needed extreme violence before they printed anything. There was poetry in their names too: Underwood, Triumph, Olivetti, Imperial, Olympia...

A manual typewriter was equipped with keys in one set of characters either non-serif Pica (10 characters to an inch) or Serif Elite (12). Just the one font, so no chance of switching over to italics, Comic Sans Plus or Wingdings. One secretary who needed to type a marketing letter to a firm in Sweden had to borrow a typewriter from the Swedish embassy.

Claudia Vickers
Engineering mathematics department, Newcastle University

'I started with an old standard typewriter. For the mathematical equations I used Greek letters and small digits which were kept in two ancient wooden boxes. I took out the character that was needed, popped it into a slot just in front of the ribbon and thumped any key hard to press it against the paper. Then I removed it, clicked the carriage up or down and inserted the next figure. It took hours.'

Manual typewriters needed regular maintenance. If you failed do this, the holes inside letters like 'o', 'd' and 'p' clogged up with ribbon fluff, and were filled in with ink when you typed them. Picking out the fluff with the bent end of a paperclip, and running over the keys with a cloth dampened with spirit or a piece of Blu Tack, was strangely satisfying. It annoys me today when faux-typewriter fonts use blocked-in characters and uneven type to make them look like 'that crazy old-style typing' because that was the kind of work only a duff typist turned out. Look at the cover of the Caitlin Moran's brilliant *Moranthology* and you will see an example of what I mean.

The most time-consuming part of typing was correcting mistakes. What a drag that was. However good a typist you were they crept in — in my case they didn't creep, they swanned in all over the page. To make a correction you needed a special ink eraser in the form of a pencil. You rolled up the paper a couple of inches, rubbed out the offending characters with the rubber at the pointy end then brushed away the detritus with a little brush at the top. Then, assuming that you hadn't gouged a hole in the paper, you rolled it back down again, aligned it with the rest of the typing as best you could, and filled in the gap where the mistake had been. Does this sound a tedious process? You're right.

A quicker solution (forgive the pun) arrived with correcting fluid. This came under various brand names, such as Snopake, Tippex and Wite-out, but was basically all variants of Liquid Paper, a product invented by one Betty Nesmith Graham. Ms Graham had three reasons to be cheerful: she was promoted from being an ordinary secretary to PA at the Texas Bank and Trust, she was the mother of Mike Nesmith of The Monkees and in 1979 she sold her Liquid Paper company to Gillette for $47.5 million.

Liquid Paper was a mix of white paint and chemicals inside a little bottle. When you unscrewed the lid you found a little brush attached and with this you applied a thin (repeat, thin) layer of the liquid over the mistake, left it to dry and then typed over it. It was an improvement on the pencil eraser but, inevitably, there were drawbacks — for example, if you didn't screw the top back on properly the stuff dried out.

Sarah Oram
Computing, London

'Snopake came in two bottles — the actual white stuff and the thinner. They were sort of like the modern day lighter fluid refill (probably the thinner was same sort of stuff anyway). We used the little bottle until it, and the brush, thickened up. Then the really messy bit was to try and slop the thinner into the little bottle, pinching same and releasing just as the thinner was poured in to get the suction right. Most of the time, it was misjudged and we'd spend the rest of the day with hands covered in white splotches.'

There was a fine art in getting just the right amount of fluid onto the paper to cover the error without slapping it on so thickly that the page looked like a blizzard painted by Van Gogh.

Patricia Robb
Ottawa, Canada

'We used to make three copies of a letter: the original, yellow for the file copy and blue for the copy you sent to people who were being copied on the letter. If you made a mistake you needed white liquid paper to correct the original, and blue and yellow liquid paper to correct the rest of the pages. Of course you had to blow to dry it before you could correct it, or it would stick to the carbon paper.

'We used so much paper. I remember as a young woman thinking it was such a waste, it would be better if they had a second bin just for the paper so it could be reused somehow. We didn't know about recycling back then, but obviously I was ahead of my time.'

The next development, which did away with the need for bottles of paint, was little sheets of paper with a white backing. You popped one of them over the mistyping, struck the wrong key again to cover it up, backspaced to type the correct one and away you went. Simple.

Now, I am sure you are wondering how, if these erasers and paint and little bits of paper made the top copy accurate (if not beautiful), the carbon copies beneath it were corrected. The rubric was that unless you were prepared to paint out each sheet of paper and wait for it to dry, you had to use that damned eraser on the copies. Please take a deep breath because I am about to confess a shameful secret. Within a few months of starting my first job I discovered that *it wasn't always necessary to correct the carbon copies* because in most cases *nobody read them*. I am sorry if this has shocked any secretaries of a nervous disposition, and hope that any copies of mine that are filed away in company archives haven't created problems for historians; but, honestly, the patience required to rub out every mistake on five carbon copies was entirely beyond me. In any case, you could always make the odd handwritten correction in the margin if you really had to. I suppose if you were a medical secretary typing something vitally important, like drug dosages, you would correct every copy, but otherwise...? Carbon paper had its own mischievous behaviour too, it had the habit of crinkling up inside the typewriter when you weren't looking, making tasteful pictures of tree branches on the copy underneath. And isn't it strange how the term 'carbon copies' is in use, by anyone 'cc'ing an email.

By the end of the 70s, most offices had moved from using manual to electric typewriters. These were much less tiring because you didn't have to hammer the keys so hard and the automated touch made the print deep and crisp and even. So electrics were warmly welcomed — except by more well-endowed women who, leaning over the keyboard to apply Liquid Paper, found they had accidentally typed a row of 'm's, 'n's and 'b's. This was commonly known as 'tit type'.

Now: Awards Time. What is The All-Time Favourite Piece of 70s' Office Equipment? Drum roll, please, while I open the envelope. By a massive vote it is... the IBM Selectric typewriter, commonly known as 'The Golfball'!

> - 'I absolutely loved that awesome IBM Selectric typewriter and thought it was cutting edge, the newest thing. I could type so fast on that. Fast typing skills were a necessity back then.'

> - 'I will never forget how excited I was when I got my IBM Selectric Typewriter with the changeable font balls.'

- 'I remember the "clattery-whirr" sound it made. I had an IBM Executive that did justified text. Bees' knees.'

- 'Oh so exciting!'

- 'I loved the IBM Golfball, especially the red one.'

- 'Loved IBM Golfballs!'

You get the picture.

What was so special about the Golfball? It was a radically different kind of typewriter. Instead of having one key for each character, it had stick in front of the type guide with a ball stuck on top of it. The ball was embossed with characters. When you pressed a key, the ball whizzed round and thwhacked the ribbon against the paper, printing it. No keys meant no more jamming: speedy typists could break the sound barrier. Also, the carriage was static and the stick and ball made the journey across the page until you hit the return key, placed for the first time to the right of the keyboard, to begin a new line. The ribbon was housed in a cartridge together with a correcting ribbon, so if you made a mistake you just backspaced, switched over to the correcting ribbon, made the correction and then switched back again to type the right character. Hoorah! Goodbye little bottles of paint and sheets of paper and damned pencil eraser — AND no more messy ribbon changes!

Strangely enough though, innovation in typewriters never extended to their protection. The covers, if they existed, were made of soft plastic and quickly became torn and grubby. Nobody made one out of quilted Laura Ashley fabric.

Today it is easy to copy, share and store documents at will, but in pre-computer days it was a much more laborious procedure. A proficient typist could produce up to seven or eight carbon copies in one go but, for anything more some sort of duplicating method was necessary.

You may remember the scene in the TV series *Mad Men* when the first photocopier is delivered to the ad agency, greeted with excited little squeals from the 'girls' in the office. I'm not sure how squealy office girls actually were in the 60s, but I am sure they would have been thrilled at the arrival of this piece of equipment. It's hardly surprising, after all it was the first piece of office equipment to have been invented in decades. Larger companies installed them during the 60s and 70s with the biggest market share going to Xerox, so much so that for a while to 'Xerox' meant to 'photocopy'. For everyone else, high-street copy shops began to spring up.

The early photocopiers were notoriously unreliable. You may remember a scene in the film *Nine to Five* where Jane Fonda struggles with one that rages out of control, burying her in piles of paper. In my experience it was more difficult to get the wretched things to print at all, and even when they did the results would lodge somewhere inside the beasts and refuse to come out. Luckily they were large enough to climb inside, and brute force with a spanner usually produced the necessary laxative effect.

Gloria Miles
Solicitors, City of London

'We had a Xerox photocopier in the basement, and one day I was down there copying some paperwork when Sir Cullum walked in and said he did not know why we were bothering with such a contraption because it would never catch on.'

Until photocopiers became reliable and less expensive, there were two other pieces of equipment available for use as duplicators:

the Banda, which could manage up to about 15 copies, and the Gestetner, which could do 100 or more. As far as I was concerned, the only good thing about a Banda was that it was named after 'B AND A', which stood for the names of the manufacturers, Block and Anderson. In the States it was called a Ditto machine. It required typing onto special paper with a glossy backing, pressed against an inked sheet like carbon paper the wrong way round. Mistakes had to be scraped off with a razor blade and then retyped, using a corner torn off the backing sheet and slipped in under the spot. The top sheet was then duplicated on a rotary machine using spirit ink with the resulting copies appearing in fuzzy pink print on paper with a very distinctive chemical smell. The whole effect was, to be honest, amateurish, so Bandas were mostly used by small businesses, schools and voluntary groups.

The Gestetner stencil machine, properly a 'cyclograph' although I never heard it called that, was ubiquitous in offices from the early 1900s right up to the 1980s, when it was put out of business by photocopiers and printers. This is how it worked.

Rowena Smith
RAF Institute of Aviation Medicine, Farnborough

'The typewriter ribbon was disabled and a thin sheet of paper coated in wax, known as a "skin" with a thicker paper backing was inserted into the machine. As you typed, the keys cut through the wax. A firm and measured pressure was required. Special pink wax correction fluid had to be used to amend any errors. When finished, the stencil was placed on a screen wrapped around a pair of inked drums, the backing sheet removed, the drums revolved and ink, spread evenly across the surface of the screen by a pair of cloth-covered rollers, was forced through the cuts made in the stencil and transferred onto sheets of paper.'

Olwen Hanson
Engineering, Yorkshire

'Gestetner duplicators needed careful management so there was sufficient ink to do the job but not too much to result in a mess (as often happened to me). I remember on occasions being asked to make simple amendments after I had typed the stencil but before it was printed, it was a tricky job to re-insert it in the typewriter without creasing the thin skin, and then to align the typing.'

You had to get the right pressure on the keys when typing the skin: too much and you punctured holes in letters like 'a' 'o' and 'p,' so they were filled in when printed; too little and it didn't cut at all. When ruling a line in the document, you were supposed to do this with a small metal spike which, if you weren't careful, snagged and tore a hole in the skin. A sharply pointed biro was safer and just as effective. And to rule a shape like a box round a table of figures you had to be extra-careful not to join up the corners, otherwise the whole thing dropped out.

*****

Telephones had a makeover in the 70s, from the heavy, old-fashioned Bakelite handsets with dials and fabric cords that tangled up like intestines to lighter plastic models in two-tones, some even with push-buttons. This was an improvement because the old circular dials made your fingers sore even if you used a pencil with an elastic band wound round the end to stop it from slipping to pull the dial round. At the BBC, and presumably other places too, the ear and mouthpieces were cleaned and disinfected once a year by ladies in smart uniforms from a company called Phonotas, later immortalised as the 'telephone sanitizers' by Douglas Adams in *The Hitchhiker's Guide to the Galaxy.*

The entire UK telephone network was connected by landlines and managed by the Post Office as a state monopoly. It seems strange today, when 95 per cent of all UK households have at least one mobile phone, that even in 1975 only 52 per cent of them had their own telephone[8]. So it's understandable that some young women found them frightening.

Rowena Smith
RAF, Farnborough

'I was absolutely terrified when I was placed in an office with a telephone which I had to answer. Bear in mind we had not had one at home for that long, probably less than six months, and then it was a party line (no, not that kind of party, it meant we had to share with another, unknown customer). I had no idea how to handle this situation and begged to return to the typing pool. What a coward, considering for the majority of my working life I did work in an office on my own.'

Sarah Oram
London

'I worked in a recruiting agency, and the way the business ran you had to ring around your clients to see whether they wanted to buy space. I hated ringing up and cold calling, so from a personal point of view that was the most difficult. Frankly I never liked phones very much, which for a secretary was a bit of a drawback.'

There was that 'secretary voice' you had to adopt when answering the phone, identifying yourself to the caller. Advertisements for jobs often stipulated 'a good telephone manner' as essential not, as one secretary I knew used to shout, 'Whatcha want then?' when her phone rang.

Using a telephone switchboard could be part of a secretary's job, either as part of her normal duties or to deputise for a receptionist. This happened to me at Kimber, and I hated that switchboard. While I was immersed in deciphering a page of Mr K's esoteric dictation, the wretched thing would flash lights and demand attention. I would lift the receiver, about to say in my best telephonist's manner, 'Good morning, William Kimber,' and then remember it was mid-afternoon. Eventually I opted for the safer but less formal, 'Hello, William Kimber' to which friends who called would chortle back, 'Hello, William Kimber.' Remember, if you want to be a secretary, you need to know what time of day it is.

It shouldn't have been difficult to operate that switchboard. It had only five lines and a few switches, but it had been designed by a Gothic novelist. Deep inside it lurked secret passages and trapdoors through which callers would appear and disappear. Having thought I'd put a call through to Mr Kimber, I would pick up the handset 15 minutes later and hear, 'Hello, this is Dennis Val Baker, yes, I am still here... waiting...' The electric typewriter had the same opinion of it as I did and manifested its loathing by furtively allowing the carriage to creep leftwards as I typed; and then, when I hit the return key, spearing it straight into the switchboard, scattering its little plastic levers and cutting off all the calls.

Michelle Metz
Bowaters, Kensington

'I found the internal telephone system confusing — I kept cutting people off. I developed nervous stomach cramps which led to the company nurse giving the boss a talking to for giving me a hard time. I left.'

Another piece of equipment which made its first appearance in the 70s was the telex machine. In the days when overseas telephone calls had to be booked in advance, sometimes by as much as a week, it was very exciting to be connected to people in other parts of the world.

Sarah Oram
Computing, London

'Twixes, and I don't mean the chocolate biscuits, was a telex machine. We always called the messages "twxs". One sat in front of a rather bulky keyboard and punched out a paper tape. This produced a long roll which sometimes had to be rolled up on a reel, before attaching one end to sprockets. Then the number of the recipient was dialled, connection made, and paper tape twitched into life and chattered itself on its merry way. If a mistake was made typing the tape, a "patch" could be typed up and edited into the roll, rather like editing film I guess. I can't remember how we found the right place, but we did. And if the telex didn't transmit, you had to find the right one from a pile of tapes on your desk and send it again. This was all there was in the pre-fax era.'

Jane Green
Manufacturing plant, not disclosed

'The telex machine was a nightmare. You had to take down the telex reply either in shorthand or in note form if it was just a response to an incoming one, create the punch tape and then try to connect and send the tape through. The telex didn't always transmit, so sometimes you would end up with lots of punch tapes on your desk. You would have to remember which one was to whom. Then, when you had sent it you needed to collect the print-offs. The top copy would go to the file relating to that customer/supplier and the carbon copy would go in the telex file — which contained a copy of every telex sent/received in date order.'

And then there was the post. In a small company somebody had the unenviable job of going to the local branch of the Post Office to buy sheets of stamps. Then, as they weren't self-adhesive, she would have to use either a wet sponge or lick them herself in order to stick them on the outgoing mail before taking it to a post box or back to the Post Office.

Larger firms used 'franking' machines. Items for posting were first weighed and the cost of posting calculated. The item was then franked, which deducted the cost from credit previously purchased from the Post Office, and stamped to show that postage had been paid.

Olwen Hanson
Textile importer/exporter, Dewsbury

'In my first job we had a franking machine, which was hand operated and very heavy. I soon learned to weigh everything before franking the envelope so postage wasn't wasted. We had to ensure there was enough ink to leave an imprint and sufficient "money" in the machine, and I remember having to carry this heavy, cast iron machine on several trips to the Post Office to pay for more. In my second job, a similar company, the franking machine was more modern, it had auto-feed. Still needed to be taken to the Post Office but, as this involved driving into town, the boss's son had the task.'

*****

Lastly, clothes. The 70s has become notable, if not notorious, as the decade that fashion forgot. But before we look at what our secretaries were wearing then, I'd like to turn the clock back further to the late 1950s for what, to me, is an extraordinary account.

Heather Pippins
Johnson and Johnson, Slough

'J & J was a privately-owned company, owned by General Johnson. You were issued with a uniform. It wasn't a uniform like you think of it, it was a very pretty dress with a Peter Pan collar, little sleeves, flared pleated skirt; all very attractive. At each level in the company the girls wore the uniform in a different colour so that if the General turned up he would know exactly which part of the company you were in. They had yellow, green, red, a pale blue, and on the top floor where the Chairman and the Company Secretary and the Finance Director were, and which is where I was situated, we were navy blue, which is one of my favourite colours. Nobody minded what colour you wore, we were just all glad to have something to wear that we didn't have to provide ourselves. This was the 50s, you know. Somebody was willing to give us something to wear, and you didn't have to worry about what you were going to wear to the office because you came in in just whatever you wanted and changed. They gave us three dresses each, and they laundered them too.'

I hadn't heard about secretaries wearing uniforms before. As far as I am aware, in the 70s it was and individual choice about what to wear to work, as long as it could be described as 'presentable' or 'smart'. Generally this meant dressing more traditionally than popular fashion dictated, in classic styles and subdued colours.

Advice written for secretaries stressed they must wear neat and clean clothes; ignoring the fact that most readers lived in bedsits or shared flats, took washing to the local launderette at the last possible moment and had limited access to ironing boards. Margery Hurst, the owner of a secretarial agency, advised her clients to have three outfits: a suit with a shirt underneath that could be changed if necessary for an evening function, a dress, as long as it was comfortable, and a pinafore worn over a shirt or sweater. Never wear black, she said, because it showed the dust, or white, because it showed the dirt[9]. Helen Gurley Brown, the author of *Sex and the Office,* advised girls to go for charcoal wools and plain black with the occasional flash of strong colour, because men loved colour, and to wear clothes sufficiently figure-hugging to catch their eye[10].

PAs dressed in suits, or a jacket with a dress, or blouse and knee-length skirt; the younger ones might have turned up their hems by a few inches. Shoes would have small kitten heels, and in colder weather they added what was known as a 'good' wool coat. Two PAs told me they wore white gloves to work every day right up to the end of the 70s. As for underwear, there was always Marks and Spencer, although a trainee on a PA course was instructed to wear a Playtex bra because it provided good support and a flattering shape.

For the rest of the secretarial hierarchy, office wear was less formal. A mini-dress, or skirt with blouse from Marks, British Home Stores or C & As was the norm until mid-decade when longer maxi-skirts came into fashion. I wore plain short skirts in corduroy or (shudder) Crimpeline with cotton blouses and cardigans or jumpers. Later in the decade I gravitated to Laura Ashley's floral Victoriana and wore out a couple of pairs of knee-length boots. Miniskirts left no option other than tights for wearing underneath, even on hot days as bare legs were considered appropriate only for lolling around in the back garden or on holidays.

Amanda Lunt
London
'One hot summer's day around 1970, a pair of female twins in their late teens who were mad about fashion and always dressed identically, were sent home for wearing hotpants (basically very short shorts) even though these garments would have proved considerably more decorous when bending down to retrieve something from a filing cabinet than the miniscule skirts they normally wore.

'Maxi skirts had crept in by the winter of 1970, which, combined with a pair of warm, textured tights helped to keep the chill off those miniskirted legs: I was very proud of my dark-green, military style maxi coat, which together with a faux fur hat from Galleries Lafayette in Regent Street, and a pair of leather kneeboots, made me feel like a refugee from *Dr Zhivago.*'

Christine Allsop
Chesterfield

'People would probably only have about four or five outfits to wear for work. They tended to wear the same clothes for a couple of days. You were considered very odd it you wore something different every day. No one was that elegantly dressed, there was not the money or the clothes available in the shops. I'm talking northern England not Paris.'

Offices in the 70s were riven by the hot topic of whether women should be 'allowed' to wear trousers to work. It may be difficult to appreciate now why it was such a contested issue, but traditional employers firmly believed that trousers on women were not 'smart' and some were quite prepared to send anyone who arrived wearing them straight home. A senior BBC secretary, who had been wearing trousers to work for some months without attracting comment, was refused entry to a posh departmental tea party when she turned up in a pair; and at Yorkshire Television a dispute arose which took seven hours of talks to resolve, and only ended when agreement was reached that women could wear trousers providing 'high standards of dress were maintained' [11].

Even secretaries themselves were divided on the matter. Many older ones had never worn trousers at home, let alone to work: one told me she was 22 years old before she bought a pair. Among younger secretaries though, trousers seemed a practical option. They had the advantages of warmth and modesty over miniskirts, as well as concealing legs that shorter hems cruelly exposed. By the end of the decade the trouser ban was generally being relaxed, usually starting with a rule that they could be worn if they were part of a 'trouser suit'. However, one secretary remembers there still being a ban on wearing them in the 1990s at a county town solicitors' office.

Valerie Docker
Temporary secretary, London

> 'When I first came to Britain from New Zealand you were expected to wear a nice dress, but I also had some smart trouser suits. I would come in as a temp, you know, a wee bit off to the side, in my trouser suit, and they would look at me but not say anything. This would encourage the other women, Oh well, if that temp can wear trousers so can I. So I think there were a lot of firms that I gradually nudged into changing their ideas.'

An emphasis on 'high standards of dress' at Yorkshire TV and elsewhere could lead to misunderstandings.

Deirdre Hyde
Publishing, London

'The times were slowly changing. Biba had opened their store in Kensington High Street, and I turned up on my first day in yellow trousers and a cotton patchwork blazer, with a really natty pair of co-respondent shoes. The Personnel Manager had a quiet word with me and I got the spring coat out again.'

Lucy Fisher
Publishing, London

'I once turned up in a striped ticking flying-suit with the legs rolled up over pink fishnet tights, with a hole in the knee where I'd fallen over thanks to the pink lace high heels. I know, I know, I should have rolled the legs down. I was still trying to be bohemian. What a twit.'

Denise Tomlinson
BBC, London

'In my late teens I prided myself on wearing the latest fashions (within my budget – usually from Chelsea Girl) and had long permed curly hair as was the trend. I was somewhat taken aback at the end of my assignment to read in my appraisal that my work was excellent, despite my 'scruffy' appearance! I think she'd have preferred someone in a twinset and sensible shoes.'

I wonder what was said about the secretary I knew who used to turn up at work in a series of ballgowns. And of course, even if an employer didn't like what you were wearing on top, he had no idea what was going on underneath.

Debbie Maya
BBC, London

'We wore what we liked. I wore maxi dresses or cords. Wedge shoes. In the hot summer of 1976 I wore no knickers.'

Chapter 4 : A wife without the love

Having established the practicalities of secretarial work, let's move on to the way in which the popular media portrayed secretaries. How were they seen in films, cartoons, newspaper articles and on TV, and how accurately were they depicted?

Search online for images of 1970s' secretaries and you will find plenty of coiffured, well-dressed women sitting at desks with a telephone or pencil in their hands, while suited men stand around looking stern and authoritative. Some might remind you of Miss Moneypenny from the James Bond films — they might even be Miss Moneypenny. This type of mature, poised and well-dressed woman fits the profile of an 'office wife'. To us, she will be useful in examining the relationship that was critical to every secretary: that between her and her boss.

The term 'office wife' first appeared in America and became widely known after a popular novel with this title was published in 1930. It originated from the assumption that women, by their nature, could only derive personal satisfaction through supporting a man and helping him to be successful. This was the role of a wife, and therefore too of a secretary. They shared the same attributes: physical attractiveness, calmness, loyalty, tact and efficiency. The only difference between the two was that a secretary also had to be emotionally detached, to be a 'wife without the love'.

That some bosses accepted this as the norm is apparent from these comments, collected by Rosalie Silverstone in the early 1970s:

> - 'It is a theory of mine that a secretary is an extension of a businessman's wife. The secretary does in the office

what a wife does in the home, from a backing-up point of view.'

- 'She is a logical extension of me, therefore I expect her to volunteer to operate in all activities in which I operate. She is like a detached member of the family.'

- '[She is] a wife in the business sense – someone to look after me.

--'A secretary should have an admiration for her boss and then she would be a better secretary."[12]

-'She has to do all those things which I have neither time nor inclination to do.'[13]

The characteristics of an office wife are described most vividly in the handbooks written to advise secretaries, two examples of which, Violet K Simons' *The Awful Secretary's Handbook* and Dorothy Neville Rolfe's *The Power Without the Glory,* were in circulation in the 1970s. Both, while including practical information on matters such as how to address a letter to an Archbishop and the meanings of legal and financial terms, devoted chapters to the necessity for good presentation, efficiency, respect, confidentiality, loyalty and tact. A secretary should always identify her boss's needs and attend to them without question or complaint. If she was having a bad day she should keep it quiet although he was to be permitted his bad moods and irritability. She must never bother, criticise or belittle him. Above all, it was her job to be useful to him.

But how many secretaries actually read these handbooks? Most contributors answered that, although the reference material had been useful, the pages about behaviour were 'out of touch with the real world', 'tripe,' and 'we had a laugh at them'. They didn't feel a book had been necessary to tell them how to conduct themselves at work, after all, the right attitudes had been implicit from the start of training. Commonsense was seen as being much more valuable than anything in a book.

So how accurate an image was the office wife? Were secretaries subservient? Would they do anything to be useful to the boss? Was it true, as popular fiction often suggested, that they always fell in love with him? What if the two of them didn't get on, what happened then? And were there situations in which the description simply couldn't apply?

*****

First point, power. However companionable a boss and secretary were, and whether they were the only two members of staff or served in a company of 10 or 20 thousand, they were never equals. He was in authority and his secretary deferred to him. This underpinned everything else, and if you were a secretary you simply had to accept it in order to make anything of your job. However, you were not his only inferior, any man who reported to him was too. The difference in your case was that your deference was fixed because it was based on your gender.

That said, let's consider the qualities that Neville Rolfe and Simons stressed as being essential for secretaries and see how far they applied. The first was efficiency. A PA had the tough job of being both 100 per cent efficient in her work while remaining utterly courteous and professional in all her dealings. The same was expected at lower levels, but general secretaries tended to have less contact with people at the top of the company and could be more relaxed. Providing she typed fast and accurately, could read her shorthand and showed enough commonsense to keep the office rolling along, she was efficient. Repeatedly, bosses told Silverstone that a good secretary was invaluable: a bad one was worse than none at all. 'A man with a bad secretary is only 60 per cent efficient ... with a bad secretary I have to do 40 per cent more work,'[14] said one.

What the handbooks omitted was the other side of the coin. An efficient boss made a secretary's job much easier; those who kept changing their minds or making mistakes created a lot of extra work and resentment. Some contributors did not subscribe to the advice of never correcting the boss.

Valerie Docker
Not disclosed, London

'Some of the men you worked for weren't as bright as buttons. There was one ...there were some basic things I had to tell him. He was writing to somewhere like Bhutan and he said, "As you are a member of the Commonwealth you can do this, this and this," and I had to say, "No, they're not!"'

Sarah Oram
Computing, London

'There were people who'd want to nit-pick and send work back to you. I can think of one particular guy who, instead of writing his amendments on what you'd typed, would go back to his original draft and the first amendments were done in blue, the second were in red, the third were in green. After a while you'd take the corrected draft, say "Thank you," type it again and not alter anything, and when you handed it back to him, he'd go, "Oh yes, this is much better now." Some were just power playing. You thought, "Oh, grow up". It was a bit frustrating when you could do the work better than they could.'

Respect was another important factor, secretaries were expected to show this at all times. An intriguing side to this is the ways that bosses and secretaries spoke to each other. Watching a series of the TV advertising drama *Mad Men,* set in the 1960s, I was very surprised that the secretaries spoke to the bosses like eager schoolgirls. Perhaps in the States, and in an earlier decade, that was the norm, or perhaps that was how the production team wanted them to be portrayed. In the UK, until the early 1970s it was still common for bosses and secretaries to maintain some distance by using 'Mr' and 'Miss' — there weren't many 'Mrs's.

Sheila Shaw
Children's charity, London

'In my first jobs in the 1950s, relationships were more formal and surnames were used between me and my bosses. Later, from the 1970s to 1990s it was much more relaxed and first names were used.'

Chris Green
BP, Feltham, Middx.

'In the 60s you certainly wouldn't call your boss by his first name, it was 'Mr'. Definitely.'

A more old-fashioned attitude was to ignore a woman's married status completely, as in this case.

Gloria Miles
Solicitors, City of London

'Sir Cullum made an effort to speak to all of the staff when he was in the building and was always very friendly and interested in how we and our families were. When I got back to work after my wedding I passed him in the corridor and he said "Ah, Miss Daniels, how was your honeymoon, enjoyable I hope," and until the day I left he always referred to me as Miss Daniels.'

Confidentiality had always been at the heart of a secretary's job. A PA had to be completely trustworthy because she would read, type and circulate documents which might be of national or commercial importance or refer to matters the management wanted to keep from other employees. At all levels, secretaries quickly learned how to identify what could and couldn't be revealed to whom.

Mary Ankrett
PA, Printing company, Walsall

'I felt that the relationship I had with my boss was what one should expect. I was trusted to keep everything I knew confidential. Because of my position I knew much about the company politics, finance, what was happening in the business, information about various members of staff. If I learnt things which he ought to know he expected me to tell him, which I did, although I made a rule of my own that I would never tell him anything which I could not prove. One could say we had a mutual understanding and respect for each other, but I would not say it was a partnership, more of team working.'

Hazel Channon
Soft drinks company, Chelmsford

'I was secretary to the legal advisor, one of four who wanted a management buy-out. I fully understood the discretion that was needed but it was extremely stressful, and at times I did feel I was not fully qualified for the job. The merger had to go to the Monopolies Commission, so once it got to the final negotiating stages it was prudent practice for senior personnel from Canada Dry and Britvic to meet away from both headquarters. My boss and I travelled to hotel venues in order that the press would not stumble on the fact that it was about to take place, if they had got wind of the merger they would have had a field day.'

Sarah Oram
Computing, London

'Confidentiality? Yes, all the way along. Some of the time I worked in Personnel Departments, so you were handling confidential information, such as salaries and appraisals and any problems that might come up. And sometimes government contracts that you couldn't talk about anyway. Frankly, you didn't go around saying "Ah hah! I'm dealing with confidential stuff," you were just discreet.

'There were a couple of things that I disagreed with totally when I was working for a guy I didn't like at all. I did possibly pass some information down the line which I shouldn't have done, and that person was very grateful for it. Looking back on it now I still think, "Yes, I was justified in doing it", because frankly this person was trying to do this other person out of something they should have had. There wasn't any comeback because he never knew anything about it.'

Loyalty was another essential ingredient. Secretary and boss often formed a close unit and it was common for her to protect and cover for him.

Phyllida Scrivens
Various, London

'Often they needed protecting from the press, embittered individuals, stalking women, top floor managers. I learnt how to tell callers that he was simply not available and that I would tell him they called; even when he was sitting on the chair next to my desk.'

Deirdre Hyde
Publishing, London

'Telling untruths to protect my boss usually involved saying (on the telephone) he was out of the office or in a meeting, that sort of thing. There were one or two occasions when he returned from a long lunch very much the worse for wear, and I would provide coffee and hide him from anyone who mattered.'

Sue MacCulloch
Northwick Park Hospital

'I have done, yes, protected consultants or the lower ranks of doctors from patients phoning and saying, 'I must speak to him...." I'd say "Sorry he's not available, he's in a clinic," when he was sitting next to my desk drinking coffee — but obviously only if he's sitting there going [whispers] "No! No!"'

Contact, which originally meant meeting or writing 'with tact', formed a large part of a secretary's job; so she had to be tact-ful. This meant dealing appropriately with people at all levels inside and outside the company; it was important not to be officious, demanding or servile. According to Neville Rolfe, you achieved tact by being unselfish, empathetic and imaginative. Simons provided guidance for what to do if, when the boss bent down to pick something up from the floor, he broke wind; which was that his secretary should immediately enquire whether he had injured his back, assist him to his chair — and not laugh until she was back in her own room.

Sadly, while the secretary was exuding loyalty and tact, it wasn't always reciprocated. It was as if both boss and secretary started with a deposit of goodwill in a relationship bank which could build further if things went well, but episodes of inefficiency, disrespect and insensitivity on either side depleted the stock. I fell out with one boss when he insisted my planned annual leave had to be cut short by a few days so that I would be back at work when he returned from holiday himself. I was there on the appointed day, awaiting his arrival, only for him to phone up and inform me that he was going to extend his trip by another week, with no apology for having messed up my plans. I left soon afterwards. I suppose it wasn't surprising that, when I saw him in a London street a couple of years later, he failed to recognise me.

There are two more qualities that I think were essential to a good boss-secretary relationship, neither of which featured in the handbooks: kindness and a sense of humour. Both appear in this little story.

Tanya Bruce-Lockhart
London Weekend Television, North London

'I had a holiday in the summer and met this dog on a beach. It had three legs and one was at right-angles. I managed to find a vet, got the dog in a splint and after about three weeks it came back to me in England. I was living in Notting Hill Gate in a little two-roomed flat and I thought, this dog has been through a trauma, it's been on a beach, it's been on a plane, it's been stuck in quarantine, I can't leave it in my flat all day. So I started taking the dog, Rikki, into the office and everybody was perfectly comfortable with it, he'd sit under the table and I'd take him out at lunchtime. He was never on a lead but he was a very patient, good dog.

'Anyway, there was an admin man, and I was summoned to his office and he said, "Look, Tanya, if you continue to have this dog everybody will bring in their dogs, cats, grandmothers, you cannot have this dog, it's just not possible. You'll have to make other arrangements." Now, I'm not good at taking No for an answer, so I went back to my boss, Frank [Muir[15]], and said, "I'm sorry, but it's either me and Rikki, or neither of us. I can't leave the dog locked up all day."

'He said, "Wait a minute." And he wrote a memo to the then Chairman of LWT saying, "Tanya Bruce Lockhart's popular pet, imported from southern Spain, was believed to be of canine origin but when she got it out of quarantine and introduced it to her vet, the vet said in fact it wasn't a dog at all but a rare species of Hornless Andalusian Goat, and I don't think there is anything in the working regulations at London Weekend Television that says, No goats.

'The Chairman wrote back to Frank, "Yes, I've seen the goat in the corridor, it's a very amiable beast, you must keep the goat. It can be a mascot to the company." So after that, in all my contracts was written, "Tanya Bruce Lockhart and The Goat Rikki". And he went everywhere with me. I mean, it's ridiculous that one should even take the dog into account, but it wasn't an affectation, it just became one of those things that people accepted, and nobody else brought their dogs or their grandmothers in.

'Frank was a thoroughly nice man, and everything you saw of Frank was what he was, there were no sides to him.'

Tanya obviously enjoyed working for Frank Muir, as I did for my last boss, Louis Marks.[16] He was a BBC television producer who had written for and edited episodes of *Dr Who, Doomwatch* and numerous other dramas. He was courteous, appreciative, and, best of all, willing to discuss whatever he was working on, using me as a sounding board, much as John Parry had done previously. On my first day he greeted me with, 'In this business everyone's opinions count, so if you see something that's is wrong, or you have an idea for the programme, tell me.' What an offer! He kindly listened to all my suggestions, patiently explaining why they wouldn't work. As a result I learned a great deal about writing, film and theatre from him. He had a dry sense of humour — his definition of a pessimist was 'a man who puts prunes on his All-Bran' — and a self-deprecating humility that masked a ruthless commitment to making the best possible programmes. A happily married man with a charming wife and two lovely daughters, we kept in touch until his death in 2010. Some of my fondest secretarial memories are of quiet afternoons when Louis and I worked on steadily in adjoining rooms, occasionally answering each other's questions, telling each other jokes and stories and sharing his favourite macaroons during our tea break.

Other secretaries too formed very happy working relationships with their bosses.

Valerie Docker
BBC World Service, London

'He was a really nice, kind, funny, lovely sort of guy and I could see why his secretaries usually stayed with him because he did involve you, he did talk to you as if you were a human being, which shouldn't be unusual but it is. He could tell me a few things and say, "Don't tell anyone," because they were staff matters.'

Andrea Sarner
TV company, London

'We had a friendly partnership, though they were always the boss. I think it worked pretty well, though I'm not sure if today's young women would think so. The best was a really funny and also considerate guy, he'd try to make me laugh just when I was about to speak on the phone. The worst was an older guy who bored me senseless with his war stories.'

'Olwen Hanson
Engineering, Yorkshire

'[My boss] believed that people wanted two things from life: good health and a reasonable standard of living, so he made the workplace as safe and comfortable as he could and paid his employees an above-average wage/salary.

'In my first two jobs the relationship was deferential, generally unquestioning and uncritical; in the remaining ones it was more questioning, more of a partnership. With all jobs it was discreet and loyal; usually tactful and mostly unemotional.'

Judith Farnell
Various, Huddersfield

'I loved that: the close relationship with your boss, getting to know how best to help and when to back off, supporting other staff, the list is endless. My dad told me that my job was 'anything your boss asks you to do', however trivial (obviously not sexual favours though!). I was always more than happy to provide tea, entertain visitors or whatever else was needed to get the job done.'

*****

As Judith's dad advised her, a secretary had to be willing to do anything the boss asked of her. I wondered whether it was possible to estimate the level of subservience that secretaries were willing to offer by looking at demands made by their bosses to undertake extra tasks, those which were beyond their usual remit or which might be considered unreasonable.

What *was* unreasonable? That varied from job to job, from boss to boss and secretary to secretary, much came down to company custom and individual preference. Neville Rolfe recommended that renewing a driving licence and buying cigarettes were acceptable, while purchasing clothes, presents or flowers were not; but even she couldn't decide about picking up children or typing the minutes of a meeting of the parish council. The boss could always argue that his time was worth more to the company than hers and it made sense if she popped out to pick up his dry cleaning, giving him time for an important meeting. But what about her time too, to what extent was it less valuable than his?

Requests which contributors said had stretched the limits of their loyalty included: walking a dog for a member of the board, washing the walls in the tea room prior to a visit from an Important Person and having to call the boss's home to ask her housekeeper to take meat out of the freezer. Here are a few more:

Susan Weir
Media company, London

'I used to be sent round the corner to place his bets. He gave me cash as the company and the bank had withdrawn his cheque book. He would bet on anything — the next person coming round a corner, number of the next bus, etc. He always lost. He was earning top money. The company was very understanding and never sacked him. Sadly, divorce ensued but he lived to a ripe old age.'

Andy Sarner
TV company, London

'My boss asked me to feed his parking meter. I fed the wrong one and he got a ticket. My fault (at the time I blamed the meter layout). To his credit he took the parking ticket and smiled. We're still friends.'

Margaret Taylor
London Transport

'On one occasion my boss asked me to go to the local fishmonger to collect a crab that he had ordered. I willingly went, but hadn't realised that the crab would be alive! I spend the rest of the day with a live, fair size crab sitting under my desk — I think that incident is responsible for my aversion to eating crab.'

Mary Ankrett
Car dealers, Walsall

'It was at a Ford dealers who not only sold cars but also mechanical plant equipment, my boss was the manager of the Plant Department. He was a rather plump man who took snuff. He expected me to go and fetch his snuff from the local tobacconist, which I hated doing. Some of the other personnel used to laugh when I went out and say, 'Are you going to fetch your snuff?' Although I was 22 at the time, I felt like a little girl.

'I hated to hear him sniffing his snuff. He was never rude, just business-like friendly, but I was not happy. I stood it for two years and managed to find another job. When I told him I was leaving, he was a bit surprised, asked me why, but I did not tell him the real reason, I just said I wanted to progress in my career (which was true) and had found a job which enabled me to do that. I realised that working for the Plant Manager in this company was not a route to progression.'

Sharon Tagle
Brochure company, Philadelphia

'I had to watch my boss's apartment and water his plants when he went on vacation. The indignity was that he didn't ASK me, he TOLD me I was going to do this. Again, another boss, who lived two blocks from the office, would not allow me, who took a bus 15 miles one way, to leave early one day when a blizzard was predicted and it began to snow. Heavily. Other secretaries were required to plan elaborate dinner parties for their boss's families, or run personal errands for their wives. This was expected and we didn't know how or if we could refuse.

Another grey area, one in which the secretary found herself edging closer to the wifely role, was preparing and serving food — these being the days when it was assumed that women had been selected by evolution to provide meals on demand.

Sandra James
Accountants, Birmingham

'Occasionally I was expected to prepare food for visitors, perhaps ten people. The money would be refunded. Some of the secretaries would cook or prepare food at home for buffet lunches and enjoyed doing this, but not all. But they were expected to do it.'

Lucy Fisher
Publishing, London

'At Thames and Hudson, we were only invited to meetings so that we could buy and serve the food.'

Alison Chubb
Import/Export, Frankfurt

'I eventually got a job with an unconventional American who didn't seem bothered about my slow speeds and lack of sophistication. After a year, he moved his business to Germany and I went with him.

'Whereas I didn't mind doing correspondence, I resented having to do personal things for him such as ordering his cigars. He would throw very specialised documents at me and ask me to translate them. When I told him I didn't have the technical vocabulary for that particular subject he would say 'I thought you said you spoke German – just get on with it!'

'Some things were just plain unreasonable. We didn't have a kettle, cups or coffee as he was too mean to buy them, and one day a client asked him if he could have some coffee. The boss asked me to get some. The nearest cafe was several streets away. I begged the German cafe owner to let me borrow the cup and saucer (it was before the days of takeaway paper cups), promising to bring them back. I then worried that the coffee would be cold by the time I got back so I started running with it and nearly got hit by a tram!'

Ultimately tact was needed on both sides, and a boss who was appreciative, even apologetic, about asking favours would get much more out of his secretary than one who was disrespectful and demanding. Much depended on the level of goodwill in the relationship bank.

I found the most useful way of gauging the acceptability of a demand was whether I could use it to my own advantage: quid pro quo, that's how I looked at it. Hardly a mark of subservience. I spent hours taking detours on the walk back from the offices of *The Times* newspaper, having delivered letters there by taxi for Mr Kimber. The most annoying one was, in retrospect, trivial. I was asked by another boss to buy a birthday card for his head of department. What man sends a birthday card to his departmental head, I thought, stomping glumly around the stationery department of John Lewis. As my boss had taken his blonde, miniskirted and very bright former secretary out to lunch, I had a strong suspicion that I had been sent on the stupid quest to get me out of their way. I chose a very expensive card. I was never asked again.

*****

Far more popular than the handbooks have been novels in which secretaries seduce or are seduced by their bosses, all those steamy affairs between the ruggedly handsome Head of Regional Sales and his temptress of the typewriter. Since the 1890s, the erotic potential of the boss/secretary relationship has been fuelling an industry of cheap novels, each valiantly trying to appeal to the 'women's' culture of the day. The 1920s saw the publication of *Money Isn't Everything,* and *Rival Wives;* the 1940s *Professional Lover* and *Heartbroken Melody. Venetian Fantasy* and *Very Private Secretary* came out in the 1950s; and the 70s saw *Promoted: Secretary to Bride,* and *Shopping for a Husband.* The genre is still going strong: *Innocent Secretary: Accidentally Pregnant, Billionaire Seduction: Surrogate Secretary* and *Hired:*

the Sheikh's Secretary Mistress are available today, should you require further reading. The cinema too has adopted the theme, from *Nine to Five, Beauty and the Boss, Hired Wife, Populaire, The Proposal* to *Secretary*. So let's have some moonlight and love and romance — we'll leave the darker side of sex to the next chapter.

If you haven't already moved on, perhaps we should begin by reminding ourselves that the secretaries of the 70s had been raised in the era of no sex before marriage, a message also repeated in the handbooks. Romance with the boss would lead only to being pitied and laughed at, said Simons, and if you couldn't avoid it, at least be sparing with the evidence. However, by the early 70s, a breezy cheerfulness about sex had appeared. Jilly Cooper, in a jolly-hockey-sticks way, thought having a crush on the boss was no problem if it lightened up the prospect of going to work, and that the occasional 'pass' was great fun. For Helen Gurley Brown, falling in love with the boss was essential to enjoying office life to the full, although she cautioned against letting things go too far: the thrills, she said, were transitory and affairs always ended badly. From the male perspective, Bernard Hollowood, in an article published in *The Observer* in 1978, depicted a secretary called 'Dorcas', whose ambition was to find a wealthy boss for a husband, preferably one who 'looks like David Dimbleby'[17]. If humorous back then, its patronising tone today suggests to me a limit to its authenticity.

But don't let's get too carried away here. When Rosalie Silverstone interviewed a group of London secretaries, only 17 per cent said they had felt a romantic attachment to their bosses, and the men too were cautious, saying they preferred to avoid 'emotional things' at work. However, Silverstone did admit her respondents may not have been telling the whole truth.

Contributors had mixed feelings on this issue.

Mary Ankrett
Printers, Walsall

'I wanted to be a professional secretary and would never have entered into any romantic situation. The man I worked for was of a very upstanding character and our relationship was, rightly, very formal. He never used my Christian name.'

Phyllida Scrivens
Various, London

'I was often in love with a boss, even when engaged or even married. It was all in my head though. In those days the relationship was very confidential, and if they were personable and friendly it was hard not to get close.'

Not all affairs ended badly, at least one had a happy ending.

Michelle Metz
Cape Asbestos, London

'When I first worked for my boss, Christopher, he had a girlfriend. They didn't live together but I think she worked for the company too, and he used to bring her to work in his car. I remember twigging what was going on and being an innocent little 19 year old I was rather shocked.

'The romance between my boss and me was a pretty slow burn, certainly on his part, I think. Things moved on a bit shortly before my 21st birthday when I was dumped by my then boyfriend (much to my mother's relief!). However it meant that I didn't have a partner, so to speak, for my dinner dance party. I asked Christopher to fill that role. Subsequently he asked me out to dinner. A bit later he asked me to go back to his flat to work on some project that had an urgent deadline and his subsequent gesture of gratitude was a kiss that was probably more passionate than warranted!

'I don't know that anyone at Cape knew that a romance was developing, except probably one very good friend who worked there for the Company Secretary. We flat-shared, so by then she would have known. When Christopher left to work for a management consultancy he asked me to go with him, so I relocated to an office in New Malden. By this time we (both young and single) were romantically involved with one another which probably explains why I would agree to reverse commute to a rather dreary building in a boring suburban setting! Lunch hour shopping opportunities were reduced to pretty much zero, unless you count Bentalls in Kingston which was a bus ride away.

'I am sure that people did know about us, but we were very discreet about our relationship and took care to keep our office and personal lives separate. I continued to flat-share with friends. In my circle it was not acceptable for unmarried couples to live together and my family would have been appalled had we done so. Christopher and I got married in the autumn of 1970 and we agreed that it would be fairer on our office colleagues if I found a job elsewhere.'

*****

If the 'office wife' is starting to look less than adequate as a description, here's a thought: was there another relationship that fitted boss-and-secretary just as well and, in some cases, better? I am thinking of those situations where the boss supported her ambitions, encouraging her to learn the business, something more like a mentor-pupil.

Kathryn Vaughan
College of Psychic Studies, London

'The President's background was so different from mine — he was from a wealthy family with a public school education, whereas my family was clearly working class. Remember we'd just come through the 60s, and I think he was dazzled by (a) the fact that I had a degree and (b) that I had uprooted myself from my family and was trying to create a 'different' life.

'The College was run in a very old-fashioned way, and when he entered the building everyone sat up a bit straighter and jumped to attention. He was referred to by senior staff as Father, though I'm afraid I thought of him as Daddy-O.

'I think he was genuinely sorry when I left in the summer of 1973. He and I kept in touch until his death and he would treat me to a lunch at his Club about once a year when I visited London.'

Jane Green
Manufacturing plant, Not disclosed

'I got on very well with my boss. Our relationship was probably unusual as we did socialise outside of work. My husband and I went to his house for dinner and he and his wife came to our house for dinner. They also came to our wedding. I think that was pretty unusual at the time. It wasn't something that I discussed with other office staff, I think they would have been horrified with the idea. I guess he was like a father figure to me.'

Jane Osborn
Not disclosed

'One boss in particular was an older man who used to give me lunch in his flat above the office on a regular basis. I think he was lonely — and there was never anything beyond that lunch. It was a more innocent time.'

*****

What about those situations where the boss-secretary relationship wasn't either satisfactory, romantic or supportive? If your guy wasn't Mr Right but Mr Wrong, or even Mr Weird? The problem here, for a generation of women whose upbringing had taught them that the men were in charge, was a reluctance to be assertive or seen as insubordinate, even 'pushy'. Violet Simons advised that this meant a choice between putting up with a bad situation or handing in your notice.

Sharon Tagle
Philadelphia

'I don't believe we were actually taught in secretarial school to assume a subservient position but again, it was implied that certain tasks and behaviours were expected and part of the position. We learned appropriate "business etiquette" and "phone etiquette" but not "dealing with a rude, demanding boss" etiquette.

'As late as the eighties when National Secretaries Day became a thing, I was executive secretary to a prominent physician at a nationally renowned hospital. He was department chairman and his wife was his assistant, so I reported to both of them. Secretaries Day came and they forgot about it. Around 4.00 pm, I guess, when they noticed all the bouquets on all the other secretaries' desks, the wife was quietly dispatched to find me something. She returned with an extremely faded large chocolate heart (I think it was sitting in a sunny store window all week) and a sad, half-deflated balloon.

'I am a little angry that I was not more assertive.'

Karen Suller
Woodbridge, Connecticut

'I was a secretary at BIC Pen in the mid to late 70s. They paid $100 per week more than any other job at the time. I was a single parent and needed the money. The employment agency told me it was "combat pay" and asked if I thought I could handle it. The anger, screaming and violence in that job was so stressful. I lasted five years then left to go to college.'

Gill Bazovsky
Public relations, London

'The new director was dishonest. He was up to all sorts of tricks, posing as Lord So-and-So on the phone. He had lots of innovative ideas that usually meant cheating other people or appealing to their snobbish natures, like wrapping paperback books with book covers that looked like tooled leather. That's the mildest example. He also encouraged people to send us money and then didn't supply the goods. He had a chauffeur who was very loyal but he was not so happy when he didn't receive his pay. It was obvious this director was a cheat, a boastful Mr. Toad. I spent a weekend worrying about how to get out of the company, then handed in my notice on the Monday and felt very relieved. But they failed to give me my back pay, despite my having been promoted to Associate Director.'

Susan Strudwick
Solicitors, Not disclosed

'At one particular practice, while my boss was away I was asked to work for the second senior partner. I went to his office and he gave me work to do, and I just said, "OK".

'He absolutely turned on me and said, "You will not say those words in this office!" Why? Because it was slang. I just smiled, took the work from him, left his office and went home.

'Next morning my own boss came back. He was such a lovely guy. He knew what had gone on and said he was very sorry. I still had to do the work, but was never asked by that particular partner again. Our tea lady, Helen, stood no nonsense though. The same partner said something to her once and she replied, 'Don't you point your finger at me!'

Christine Allsop
Quarry, Chesterfield

'The worst was the General Manager for a stone quarry business, an ex-policeman who had found religion. He was always staring at me and his desk was positioned so he could do this. When I asked why he did, he said they were taught to do this in the Police Force, it made criminals feel uncomfortable. I remember thinking, "I am not a criminal" but not saying anything. No one dared answer back in any of these positions in the 70s, it would been classed as insubordinate.

'When I eventually got another position and handed in my notice, he took me to one side and, because a number of other staff had already left because of him, begged me not to say I was leaving for the same reason. He feared that he would be dismissed. I just wanted to get away so I did not say anything. I even felt a bit sorry for him.'

Lesley Powell
Not disclosed

'When I took the job he said he was planning to expand into Europe. Well, that didn't happen. He expanded in the UK taking on a lot more staff, but they were not well supported.

'Gradually he got more greedy and was syphoning money out of the company for a personal project and in the end put it into receivership, leaving some of his suppliers in financial difficulties. He then set up another company with different directors. I didn't really realise the extent of this and how it would impact on the company, I just didn't like what he was doing.

'I know I should have got out but I had lost my confidence, and when I was offered another job I chickened out in case the new boss turned out the same.'

Sometimes other secretaries stepped in to help their colleagues.

Heather Pippins
Builders merchants, Somerset.

'When I got to work for a Vice-Chairman I had responsibilities for the juniors, and if I saw a junior being browbeaten or put upon, then it was up to me to say something, somebody had to speak up for them. You do come across it in bigger companies, in a small groups you don't. I think it's "I'm the big man-itis" — when he's probably about five foot four. It's the shorter ones who are the more bumptious.

'There was a young girl who was straight out of school and this guy was browbeating her. I came across them one day, I walked in to where she was sitting and this man, the language he was using to her ... she was in tears. I don't like that kind of thing, I don't think it's necessary. So I went to see [my boss] and told him. "Ah, right", he said, "leave it with me". Now what happened I don't know, but I did say to her a couple of months later, "How are things now?" and she said, "Better".

If you could endure it, there might be something to be learned even from these unpleasant experiences.

Gwen Rhys
Not disclosed

'My second boss was a strange man, a kind of wolf in sheep's clothing — kind, nice, Christian, understanding, but in fact an absolute B******. He was VERY clever. I saw him use some very unpleasant tactics to drive people down in business negotiations. I didn't like that but it taught me to be careful of people who appeared to be one thing and were actually another. With hindsight, a very useful skill.'

Anne Ballard
Various, London

'I'm not the deferential type and if I encountered a boss who expected it, I moved on. Unexpectedly, I found this attitude more in places like PR and advertising; much less in legal or accountancy firms, perhaps because the work required more intelligence and the bosses respected this.

The worse cases of deference would be completely unacceptable now.'

Denise Tomlinson
BBC, London

'I caused a surprise in my first assignment. I was placed with someone in BBC Pensions who was notorious and didn't keep secretaries long. With the confidence only an inexperienced 18-year-old can have, upon being asked to make him a coffee I asked if he'd washed up his mug from the last time? He trotted off meekly to rinse it out while the other secretaries in the office went ashen-faced and had a collective panic attack.'

*****

Referring to a secretary as an office wife fails to address one situation where it didn't apply, at least not in the 1970s: not all bosses were men.

I am sorry to say that at that time women bosses had a terrible reputation. They were seen as difficult, possibly because they had been particularly assertive in getting to where they were, worked twice as hard as male colleagues to prove their worth and were reluctant to delegate responsibilities to their secretaries, a common source of frustration. Some secretaries also felt that, because the usual male/female chemistry was lacking, women were less fun to work for. More than half of Silverstone's London secretaries said they would not be happy working for a woman[18].

Valerie Docker
BBC Admin, London

'She was a real micro-manager. When she dictated a memo she always began by saying, "It's from the [job title]" as if you didn't know who she was. Every time she asked me to fetch her a coffee she told me, "I want a black coffee, with cream, from the staff canteen", as if I would ever get it from somewhere else. Sometimes she even followed me into the loo, being female she could get in there to retrieve me. She really needed to have her finger on everything. She was just incorrigible.

'All the time she distrusted people and thought they wouldn't do what she needed. The papers she gave me would be splattered with these circular red 'Urgent' stickers, even though she'd already told me everything was urgent. I think it was to allow a day or so's buffer zone before the deadline ... maybe she had been disappointed in the past by a few things going wrong. She was very focussed on getting work done.

'Working for her could be very difficult and undermining, but I had enough self-confidence just to find her funny, and it didn't wound me deeply. I would go away and have a bit of a chuckle about it. I just thought well, that's her problem really, not mine.'

Sue MacCulloch
Northwick Park Hospital, Middlesex

'There was a consultant I did some typing for. She was the only one who was ever rude or illogical in what she was asking for. I think, looking back on it, it was because she had obviously had to keep her guard up all the time.'

Phyllida Scrivens
BOC, London

'Women were trickier. As the decade went on I began finding myself working for women managers, leading to power struggles, envy, bitchiness and tears. One at the end of the 1970s was younger than me, strident, ambitious, intelligent. We kept a veneer of having a good relationship but I resented her being younger and her much larger salary. We didn't really get on.'

Mary L Cryns
Legal secretary, San Francisco

'When I left Mullen & Filippi for a higher-paying legal secretary job at Bank of America Legal Department, I worked for a female attorney. She drove me nuts and was super demanding. I found myself wishing I had never left the other firm. She was probably one of the worst I worked for. Sadly, I always had more issues with females in the work world than the males. I am not sure why, to be honest. She was demanding and constantly made me run into the office and run around and get files for her and stuff.'

'Controlling', 'grudge-holding', 'a pain in the arse,' 'an absolute bitch'; you can see how popular these women bosses were. However, it's not the whole story.

Sarah Oram
Computing, London

'I worked for several women, I never had a problem with them. There seemed to be a school of thought that it wasn't a good idea to work for a woman, everyone said, "Oh, women are bitchy." I never found that, possibly because as a secretary you are not a threat. Whether that has anything to do with it or not, I always got on extremely well with my female bosses. But equally I liked working with men, I liked working in a male environment.'

Amanda Lunt
BBC, London

'I worked mostly for women, and in almost all cases found them far more rewarding to work for than men. They seem more inclined to take you into their confidence, to let you know exactly what was going on, and to encourage you in your own career (and it wasn't likely that I was ever going to be able to step directly into their shoes, a fear that some women are said to hold regarding female secretaries and PAs). Two of the younger ones became friends for life, and even if we rarely get the chance to meet up, we still exchange Christmas cards.'

Susan Coles
American company, Paris

'I did have a woman boss in my very first job in Paris and I think she felt maternal towards me. I once had a medical concern which I shared with her, and she straight away took me to the American Hospital in Paris, where I was treated at no cost to myself. I will always remember that kindness. I would not have been able to confide to a male boss in this way.'

So were secretaries really subservient office wives? Did they all look like Miss Moneypenny? She, of course, was a PA, and we've seen how their work involved a close connection to their boss's personal as well as professional lives, so perhaps it is here that the model fits best. Miss Moneypenny was very much the kind of person Ian Fleming would have come across in 1940s' offices as would Hollywood moguls in the 50s and 60s. She did have a charmed life though, didn't she? You never saw her change a typewriter ribbon.

Wendy Gough
Local planning, Midlands

'Senior secretaries of my youth did seem more like Miss Moneypenny, but none of the bosses looked like James Bond.'

Anne Ballard
Various, London

'I remember some secretaries, usually the ones working for the "Big Boss", who were almost like wives in what they did for them. It probably is not so different now.'

Chris Green
BP, Feltham, Middx

'It's almost as if... it was going further back, I'd've said that was more 50s, 60s ... I think perhaps if you were a secretary to a Managing Director... I came across one or two of those women.'

However, apart from PAs, the office wife model clearly has its limitations. It doesn't fit so well further down the secretarial pyramid, and as we can see, by the 70s it was starting to look outdated. Real relationships between secretaries and bosses were far more complex and varied than it suggests, depending more on the bank of goodwill shared between them than on her subservience to his authority. After all, even if the title of a job was 'Secretary to..,' it had its own intrinsic value and whoever took it on was employed by the company, not the individual.

Laurie McGill
3M, Dallas

'I am not sure "office wife" would describe my relationship with any of my bosses. I never fetched them coffee nor dusted their desks. Never ran personal errands for them. I basically did secretarial duties.'

Margaret Taylor
London Transport

'I suppose I was an "office wife," but I never remember being offended by this. My boss was, in my opinion, a very knowledgeable, fair and strong manager, happy to make decisions and take the rap should he make a wrong choice. I had enormous respect for him and feel that I learnt a great deal whilst working for him. I never felt bullied or undermined, he made me feel a very important part of his team.'

When I once mentioned to one of my bosses that secretaries were referred to as office wives, he snorted, 'Hah! Whoever invented that one had a bloody funny idea of a marriage!'

Chapter 5 : The sexy secretary

In 1981 Miss Moneypenny was 54 years old: at least Lois Maxwell, who played her on-screen, had reached that age. In that year's James Bond release, *For Your Eyes Only,* it seems for a brief moment as if her yearning for romance with 007 will be fulfilled as, in the form of Roger Moore, he hands her a single red carnation. But no. Her hopes are dashed yet again. He turns and presents a large bouquet of flowers to her new, and much younger, assistant.

Bond's preference neatly signals how the popular image of a secretary had mutated from the office wife to an updated version of one that was centuries' old: the ingenue. In her 70s' incarnation, as seen in the popular media, she was a young blonde, bubbly and not-all-that-bright, dressed in a tight top, miniskirt and 'kinky' boots and often referred to as a 'dolly bird'. She was a cheeky entertainment for both men and women, and very obviously a sexual object for the pleasure of the male viewer.

Her image emerged at the same time as the demand for secretaries reached a peak and a flood of female baby boomers entered the job market. Reflecting the 60s' celebration of youth, fun and spontaneity, the dolly bird image was superimposed on these young secretaries to such an extent that to the less discriminating they became indistinguishable. Advertisements for 'mature and experienced' secretaries in the Situations Vacant columns found themselves placed uncomfortably beside those for a 'chirpy young bird', a 'beautie cutie' or an "attractive young Girl Friday.' This dolly/secretary hybrid provided plenty of opportunities for humour in cartoons and patronising, popular journalism about office life. These girls were amusing, their work was laughably inaccurate and of course they only came to work to pull a wealthy boss as a husband. Consequently, as

Silverstone observed, 'Too many bosses still generalise, and think of all (or most) secretaries as "dolly birds" with little or no intelligence.[19]'

Another attraction of dolly/secretary, at least as far as men were concerned, was their potential for sexual fun. An example of this is an article written in 1973 by Barry Norman, the respected journalist and film critic. Intended to be light-hearted — as with Hollowood, nothing about secretaries written by men could ever be anything but humorous — the piece argues against equal opportunities for women by reversing the norm. Norman wouldn't, he says, employ a 'dolly chap' instead of a 'girl secretary' because that would be no fun at all. The chap would be far too heavy to sit on his knee, and you couldn't forgive a man as much as you would a girl. After all, he went on, wasn't it perfectly reasonable for a boss and his secretary to look forward to some 'mutual massage' at the end of a long day at work?[20]

Norman's approach seems blatantly sexist today. It also shows how the blurred distinction between secretary and dolly bird had created the sniggertastic stenographic sex bomb. At the time she was perfectly acceptable: and why not? Search online for images of 1970s' secretaries and alongside the office wives you will find plenty of dolly birds in offices, buxom, blonde and bored.

Did secretaries really look like that?

Mary Ankrett

'Yes, I saw some of the images, and those which were unbusiness-like did not feel true. It was often the case that secretaries were not taken seriously by some people.'

Mary L Cryns

'He, he, he, nope. Not in our office, but I'd seen pictures of that sort of thing. I don't think the offices I worked for really fit that mold at all. We weren't sitting around filing our nails or trying to look pretty. We were too busy for that.'

Gill Bazovsky

There was a dolly bird at *Tit Bits* magazine. She was blonde & buxom, lots of make-up, very revealing tops and micro-skirts, etc.

Margaret Knowles

'The men would have liked that, I am sure, but real life was not like that.'

Heather Harvey

'I have sat, bored, on many an occasion, ready to take down dictation waiting for the boss to finish a phone call or deal with some interruption, but I wouldn't say I was a young blonde dolly bird. More a blonde wanting to finish work and get home.'

Contributors agreed that only a few secretaries were actually dolly birds, whose natural habitats were elsewhere: in shops and cafes and about town, less so offices. Looking again at these photos again, I suspect the women in them weren't secretaries at all, but models. Or typists who wanted to be models.

So having separated real secretaries from dollies, how far were they available for sexual fun? It's important, if less exciting, to remember that the sexual freedoms of the 60s didn't really take hold outside fashionable metropolitan areas until later in the 70s. Secretaries tended to come from more conservative middle- and working-class families and were cautious about abandoning the traditional values with which they had grown up.

Elaine Day
London

'I remember the instructor on the BBC Production Assistant training course referring to working on location and how it was up to us (all women) whether we kept our bedroom doors locked or not. When away filming I can remember being 'eyed up' by actors and crew members and being asked for my room number — I remember laughing and shaking my head! I wasn't interested in one night stands, although there would have been plenty of opportunity. I was very young but accepted it as part of the culture at the time.

'In one office I was shocked to learn that a colleague had had an abortion as a result of an affair and the man in question never knew. In another there was a flamboyant secretary who claimed to have slept with the entire England cricket team. And in the drama department one colleague used to leaf through the actors' directory *Spotlight,* saying "had him, had him..."'

Those men fell into the trap of mistaking secretaries for dolly birds found themselves troubled by an unstable hybrid. Behind the respectable exterior, might the young woman diligently taking down shorthand notes and making cups of coffee be yearning for a sexual indiscretion?

The 70s was the decade in which the second wave of feminism became more widely discussed. In 1972, Mary Kathleen Benét, in *Secretary: an Enquiry into the Female Ghetto,* proposed that behind the sexualising of the secretary lurked a sinister purpose, a strategy developed by management to manipulate their employees which she called the 'myth of the sexy secretary'. It worked like this: by appointing secretaries who were pretty and of an eligible age and status, managers (a) kept the wages bill low and their offices pretty, (b) protected their own positions by rewarding with attractive young women those who conformed with their opinions, and (c) maintained sexual tension at work by encouraging the women to devote themselves to the men, while at the same time denying them physical relations. Offices were, she said, full of 'young girls' engrossed in sexual daydreams while frustrated fellows fantasised about what they might do with the girls. As a result offices were thrumming with erotic tension[21].

Benét was right about sex being part of the fabric of office life, but perhaps that was likely anywhere where men and women worked closely together for much of the day. Plenty of men fantasised about young women, and they were daydreaming too, although seldom about the men. And wouldn't the demand to keep recruiting new secretaries like gold stars for good behaviour eventually become unaffordable? Moreover, according to Silverstone, older secretaries were highly valued by bosses for their greater experience and knowledge.

Besides, there were time-honoured methods for coping with sexual tension, one of which was humour. As we saw in the Barry Norman article, the dominant style was from the male point of view, although plenty of women internalised it and found it funny as well. You only have to watch clips of old comedies like *The Two Ronnies* and *The Benny Hill Show* to see examples. When Silverstone mentioned to men that she was carrying out research into women working as secretaries, the reaction was predictable.

'The immediate response, almost without exception, was jocular and sexually aware. For example: "I have an excellent secretary — she fits very well on my knee," "My secretary looks after me so well that my wife is jealous", or simply, 'Can I help you with your research?[22]'

So it isn't surprising that office humour followed this dominant pattern, leaving a secretary wondering what to do if someone cracked a joke she found offensive. Violet Simon's advice was to smile and look amused so as not to embarrass the men — no matter that she might be embarrassed herself. After all, counselled Simon, men had to have their little joke, and if they thought she was broad-minded they wouldn't be frightened of her.[23].

Flirtation was another way of releasing sexual tension. Benét claimed that secretaries had been manipulated into thinking it was better to be desired by their bosses than to aspire to become their equals, thus pressurising themselves to remain attractive and seek his 'love'. Jilly Cooper saw things in a lighter vein, and recommended companies to employ pretty girls because it cheered up the men to have someone to wolf-whistle at. She also advised any secretaries unable to keep up with their shorthand dictation to uncross and recross their legs, and those whose typing wasn't up to scratch to wear low-cut dresses and lean forwards when handing it over so the men didn't notice the mistakes[24]. Helen Gurley Brown too was all in favour of the occasional flash of an undergarment. A small-bosomed woman, she said, should wear a pretty, lacy bra with a blouse unbuttoned one below the usual; wearing a blouse and skirt wouldn't get a girl anywhere[25].

Was flirting widespread in offices?

Andrea Sarner

'I read Helen Gurley Brown's *Sex and the Office* and it was an eye-opener! I resisted the advice to undo another button on my blouse. I don't remember taking any of her advice, but it was good to read something written by somebody who actually knew what it was like to be a secretary.'

Chris Green
Chesterfield

'There was always flirting in the office, harmless flirting, like a camaraderie between everyone and you got on and it passed the day, really. That made it nicer to go into work and enjoy the experiences.'

Michelle Metz
London

'I don't recall any risqué jokes, name calling etc. in my career as a secretary. However I did become aware in my last secretarial position that my boss enjoyed having a young secretary with whom he could indulge in mild flirting, safe in the knowledge that we were both happily married.'

Sue MacCullough
London

'If somebody called you "Darling," you'd just laugh it off. It didn't mean any more than me saying to my cat, "Hello, darling."'

It was always possible that flirting would lead on to an affair. Gurley Brown suggested that every man was capable of at least one affair at some point in his life and that most single girls were willing to be a partner; even the less adventurous ones would indulge while on their quest for a husband. Helpfully, she classified office affairs between lunchtime 'matinees,' brief flings which were fitted into the working day; and more serious liaisons which might last years, disrupt careers and influence company decisions[26]. Contributors confirmed this distinction.

> - 'People snogged in the filing racks, they were married, but not to each other!'

> - 'We had the usual Christmas office party. It was an excuse to try it on with someone that you took a liking to.'

> - 'My boss and another secretary, both married to others, after a Christmas party. A great long marriage followed. Other dalliances did not last long.'

> - 'I must have lost a few pounds and learned some social skills. And smartened up. No, he didn't leave his wife.'

> - ' In summer he would bring me a single rose to the office. I had to leave as he was married with two children.'

Affairs could also lead to some unusual interventions.

> **Debbie Maya**
> London
>
> 'I saw him on a *Panorama* [BBC TV] programme, realised that he looked familiar and that he worked at Bush House, so I flirted with him and then, months later, got together.
>
> 'He was married. Interestingly the boss of my department got to hear about it, called me in and told me, "Stop it". These were the days when officials thought they could poke their nose into your business, but I was a mouthy cow so I said to him that it was not really his business, and

had he had affairs before? It didn't affect either job. I moved to Broadcasting House anyway and we kept seeing each other on and off until 1979.'

Gillian Summers
London

'Whenever Derek was in London he would travel half-way on the Tube with me and then change for Ruislip, I thought that was where his parents lived. One day, when I was standing in for the telephonist in her lunch-break, the phone rang and a woman asked for Derek. I said he was out and could I take a message. She said, "Just tell him his wife called." I was stunned. It had never occurred to me that he was married. However he dealt with it very well by asking me to meet her for a coffee in Oxford Street, when she told me that she was very lonely when he was away and invited me to go and stay with her for a weekend. We got on very well, but I lost touch with both of them when I moved to a new job.'

Inevitably though, affairs also gave rise to disappointment and heartbreak.

Andrea Sarner
London

'A (married) Vice President from America in my department used to go out with one of the other secretaries when he came to London. On one of his visits he was there when she came into my office and he froze her out. I was really embarrassed for her. I think in those days lots of executives who travelled for work would have their flings and think nothing of it.'

Jan Jones
Manchester

'I was around 20 and had been engaged for a year or so but was coming to the realisation that I had made a mistake — I was quite naive about men then.

'The chap I was working for at the time was in charge of lots of factories, as the CWS used to make all its own glass bottles, cardboard boxes etc., and a new man appeared to carry out efficiency studies at these factories. He was 27 and seemed so sophisticated to me — certainly a lot more so than my poor fiancée. He utterly charmed me, so we started to have lunchtime drinks and then went out on a couple of dates; at which point I realised that I had to break off my engagement.

'I was completely besotted with him. I think he quite liked the "power" he had over me — and I think to be honest some of that was because of my boss. There was never any bonking on the desk or anything, but there was some gossip about the number of times he visited my office. I thought we were a huge item, until after a few months he announced he had got a job in Ibiza. I was heartbroken but angry. I went off to be an air stewardess with BOAC — anything you can do, buddy — but I hated it so came back to Manchester and the CWS as fast as I could. The romance/obsession continued on and off for years to be honest — not one of the best decisions I ever made. But then again neither would it have been to have got married.'

Sharon Tagle
Philadelphia

'There was a rumor in the admin department of a prominent not-for-profit, where I worked as executive assistant, that the President was having an affair with the department receptionist and he fired her. She kept threatening to reveal their affair to his wife and the community (he served on several boards). I actually took an anonymous phone call from a woman threatening to "tell everything" unless certain conditions were met.

'Was I supposed to take a message for this? What was I supposed to do? I ended up going into his office, closing the door and briefly describing the call. He shook his head and said, "There's a lot of loonies out there."

Christine Allsop
Chesterfield

'The outcome was always painful. The men were always married and the women were always getting pregnant.'

But not everyone went that far. One boss told me most men thought about having sex with the women they worked with but were far too anxious about the consequences to do anything about it. And, as one of Silverstone's bosses put it,

'I tend to choose a secretary for her physical attractiveness, although really I should not do so because it is too threatening. After all, one spends more time with one's secretary than one does with one's wife. A man in this company got involved with his secretary and she blackmailed him. He lost his job and his home as a result, so I made up my mind never to allow this to happen.[27]'

Although it isn't clear whether he meant avoiding an affair altogether, or simply the consequences. The potential for sexual liaisons at work could also lead to comic misunderstandings.

Tanya Bruce Lockhart
London

'On one occasion, Cyril Bennett, who was a wonderful Controller of Programmes, had recently employed a young investigative journalist to work on news programmes. Cyril said to me, "I don't understand this young man, he doesn't say much."

"I've seen him around," I said, "he looks like a touring version of John Denver," — this young man he was always in kaftans, Dr Scholl sandals and granny glasses.

"Just go and talk to him."

'It was the period of hotpants and thigh-boots and I had this flowing blonde wig, I used to hide the grips with a variety of different colour chiffon scarves, but it was de rigueur, it was what lots of people were wearing. So I went into the young man's office. I was probably dressed in a short skirt or hotpants or whatever. I didn't think, "Gosh, I'm trying to do a number", I just asked him if he had found somewhere to live, had he had someone take him round the studios, just blathered on. Then I said, "Look, you and I are probably never going to work together cos you're a journalist and I'm seconded to Arts and Documentaries, but if we should work together there is something you need to know, because it's very important about my work association with this company."

'He looked me straight in the eye and said, "I never have affairs with people I work with."

Bearing in mind I was dressed as I was, I thought, "Oh God! Either I say, That's good because nor do I, or I say, That's a pity because I do!"

'My mother always said, "Tell the truth". So I said, "Well, that's fine, because what I was going to say was, that as part of my association with London Weekend Television I have a dog called Rikki, and as it's an open-plan office you will see him running around."

'He said, "What do you mean, a dog?"

'I said, "A dog. Well, actually, it's a goat."

'He said, "What do you mean, a goat?!"

'And he never got over the fact that I had made him look ridiculous by saying he never had affairs with people he worked with.'

*****

We might accept that a level of sexual attraction, daydreaming, humour, flirtation and romance was inevitable when men and women were working closely together, and that it might lead to consensual sexual relationships. But what about those that weren't? The 70s has acquired a dark reputation as the decade when sexual harassment was common in the workplace and women suffered from intimidation and humiliation without any remedy. The truth, as ever, is more complicated than this suggests.

The term 'sexual harassment' originated in the late 60s in academic circles in the United States. It took a decade to become common currency in the UK. Neither of the handbooks by

Neville Rolfe or Simons refers to the behaviour it describes, nor do Benét or Silverstone, all of whom published their work before the mid-70s. This is not because it wasn't happening but because, undefined, it didn't exist. In fact when the description was first used in the UK, it was greeted with blank stares and mild amusement as these two cartoon captions, supposedly the words of a boss to his secretary, reveal.

> "Sexual harassment? Because I admired your notebook?"

> "Let's come to an understanding, Miss Garrett. If I sexually harass you, you have the right to sexually harass me back.'

But, as one contributor put it, 'there was no joke about it.'

Sexual harassment, as defined in England today, includes unwanted behaviour of a sexual nature which violates dignity, makes the victim feel intimidated, degraded or humiliated or creates a hostile or offensive environment. In the 70s it was assumed that wolf whistling, personal remarks and suggestive jokes were part of normal banter, at least at the lower levels of office life. They were often unwelcome but not unusual, some women found them flirtatious, others offensive. And just as flirtation might lead to an affair, they created an environment in which some men felt encouraged to pursue other, more serious forms of harassment, such as persistent, unwanted attentions, gropings and so on — physical assault being, as ever, illegal. How far dolly bird images encouraged the more gullible guys to take their chances is impossible to know, but their prevalence, and the sexualising of the media in general, presumably had some effect. Not that it excuses anyone, but I wonder how many men brought up during the Second World War and its aftermath, when nice girls said No and social conventions were more restrictive, must have seen those images and wondered if they had been offered a new lease of life.

Evidence that attitudes changed during the 70s comes from a Marplan survey of working women conducted in 1982. The results found that harassment was most prevalent in male-dominated organisations, and that divorced and separated women, rather than young girls, were those most likely to attract unwanted male attention. The majority of respondents (83 per cent) said they would report an incident of harassment to a superior, but fewer (77 per cent) would do so if the firm was dominated by male employees; only 4 per cent of full-time workers said they would change job because of it. The behaviours which women found most offensive were: persistent sexual advances (95 per cent), wandering hands (94 per cent) and dirty jokes (45 per cent), with those most offended by dirty jokes being older women in higher social classes.[28] These results suggest that opinions had shifted significantly as sexual harassment had become more clearly defined and better understood.

Most of the contributors had been aware of this change in attitudes and their accounts show an interesting and credibly balanced spectrum of opinion. First, and perhaps surprisingly to some, a fair minority thought far too much had been made of sexual harassment. Either they had never encountered it themselves or only as inoffensive or non-threatening behaviour.

Judith Farnell
Huddersfield

'Working in a garage, it was pretty much a male environment. We used to run the gauntlet of whistles and calls from the lads if we had to go out of the office into the workshop for anything — in those days we called it flirting. Not that I wouldn't flirt at work — but you need to be careful how you do it. Always be polite but stand your ground, has been my motto. I was a secretary all my working life, never had any unwelcome attention, never been intimidated, but if I had had, even as a shy young woman, I would have fended it off, and if I couldn't, no matter how much I needed a job, I would have left. I value my self-respect.'

Sharon Tagle
Philadelphia

'I was never harassed or recall any sexual innuendo with anyone who directly supervised me. I may have been more naive then but I don't recall any.'

Chris Green
Feltham

'I never felt harassed. In those days it was the environment that we worked in, they would think nothing of pinching the secretary's bottom. That makes it sound as if they were all going round doing that, it wasn't the case. It was just the norm in the 70s, and you didn't think anything of it. You didn't take any notice.'

Tanya Bruce Lockhart
London

'Looking back from now, there were perhaps men who behaved, in contemporary terms, inappropriately, but you dealt with it. They might put their arms around you and give you a hug, or they might say, "Gosh, your skirt's a bit short", but you'd say, "Oh, push off". I never found it intrusive. Maybe I was rather naive, and because I wasn't looking for it I wasn't aware of it. It certainly didn't come into my consciousness that those sort of things were going on. I was never aware of anything inappropriate.'

Sarah Oram
London

"I had a boss who was very physical, but he was like that with everybody, male or female. He'd pat you on the back, pat you on the knee. It didn't mean anything. He was a really nice guy.

'There was always the Handsy Office Guy, and to be perfectly honest it didn't bother me. I'm not shy and retiring and I'm quite big, so I can intimidate people if I want to. But there was always someone who would get picked on and have a hard time and would end up in tears. We were good about supporting them and taking up cudgels on their behalf. It was pointless going to HR because they would take the side of the man, so you dealt with it in your own way.

'It sounds dismissive now, but it was taken much more lightly then. If you think about some of the gropings we put up with they would be called an assault now, but then it wasn't assault, it wasn't that serious. It was accepted that the men would try it on and that you would laugh it off, or you made sure you weren't alone in the room with that person. You would be told "You like it really," or, "Don't be silly, it's just messing around". It was dismissed on the man's side and so, frankly, it was best to do the same on yours too.

Margaret Knowles
Wolverhampton

'I think men knew whether they could or could not. I did not know anyone that had to deal with a "situation". It either never happened or they kept it to themselves.'

In my own case, I worked in about 16 different jobs throughout the 70s and ran into difficulties with only one boss. I'll tell you what happened because these incidents are typical of the kind of thing any secretary might have had to deal with.

For a short while I worked for a man, middle-aged, married, not attractive physically (to me) but intelligent and interesting. Although we got along well together, he was given to making provocative remarks in front of people which I realise now were probably designed to embarrass me and test their, or possibly my, reactions. One of my duties every day was, as usual, to fetch tea and coffee for us, and every few weeks he would give me money to use as a float. His party piece was to wave a £5 note in the air in front of visitors, saying loudly, 'Thank you my dear for a wonderful evening.' Oh, how they chuckled. It was silly and, after a few repetitions, boring; but it amused him. Being somewhat innocent, although I guessed it had a sexual connotation I wasn't entirely sure what he meant. When I told another secretary about this she was horrified and advised me to complain at once. Does he really mean what I think he means, I asked? Yes, she said, it does, and it isn't funny. I didn't think it was funny either, but then, as I had been the butt of the joke several times, it seemed too late to do anything about it by then. Anyway, I didn't want to appear prim. As the handbook said, 'Men must have their little joke'.

A second incident occurred when, wearing a shorter than usual dress, I bent over to pick up a couple of files from the bottom drawer of a cabinet. I could hear him muttering something to a male visitor behind my back and, although I wasn't able to catch what was being said, guessed the gist of it from their snorts and giggles. I felt very uncomfortable because I liked working for this man but he was destroying my respect for him. As soon as his colleague had left, I gave him a filthy look. He realised he had upset me, apologised and never did it again. At least, not with me.

On my last day working for him, he took me out for a posh lunch at a nearby bistro, bottle of wine and three courses, at which I learned how to eat an artichoke and we discussed the novel, *Clayhanger.* Returning to the office, never having previously laid a finger on me, he cornered me by the filing cabinet and lurched into a kiss; more peck than passion, but still a surprise. Who knew Arnold Bennett could be so arousing? Ah! — of course, I was leaving. There was no point in complaining, I doubted anyone would have taken me seriously. But I was shocked. It spoiled the last moments of what had been a good working relationship.

Although this man was, in work terms, senior to me, it never occurred to me that at a personal or moral level he was my superior. I felt his behaviour had let him down and that I was justified, in the second case, in objecting to it. But I never felt that I was a victim. As I said, he was the only boss with whom I had any problem of this kind, and one out of 16 hardly suggests that offices were dens of debauchery. In my experience, men were too focussed on their work to have time to harass women.

However, a 70s' secretary wanting to complain about sexual harassment faced particular difficulties. The first, as we saw from the cartoon captions, was a lack of understanding and, without any legal guidance, it was her decision alone whether the behaviour that she had found offensive would be viewed by others as serious enough to merit the complaint. It wasn't until the Sex Discrimination Act of 1975 that a woman could sue in respect of sexual harassment at work, and even then she would only be successful if she demonstrated that her treatment had differed from that towards a male employee.

If a secretary did decide to raise a complaint she had to decide where to take it. A senior manager? The personnel department (if one existed)? Who would understand the situation and act on it to her satisfaction? There were managers who would step in without hesitation to reprimand a man who didn't treat females with respect, but they tended to treat such complaints as being personal matters between individuals, and while a woman boss might be more understanding, there were few at senior levels. The perpetrator almost always had greater power and status than the complainant and the case would depend on her word against his. So our secretary would be told she had a different sense of humour to the man, or she had misunderstood his intentions. She might be told she had been 'hysterical' or 'over-reacting,' even that she had provoked the incident herself by the way she had dressed or behaved. Worse, the fact that she had made a complaint could lead to her being ostracised, even dismissed. In such an environment, it is hardly surprising that women did not feel confident enough to 'make a fuss'. Instead, the most common solution was to leave and find another job; less stressful and much simpler. More of a dilemma if you wanted to stay with the employer; and of course it left the perpetrator free to offend again.

Secretaries developed strategies for avoiding potentially risky situations.

Phyllida Scrivens
London

'Taking dictation was obviously part of the job, but somehow I always felt exposed during those one-on-one sessions behind closed doors. I made sure that as soon as the letters were done I stood and left the room.'

Anne Ballard
London

'In a couple of offices there were men one was advised to avoid, they were both in lowly positions like the despatch room and picked on the young and vulnerable girls who couldn't deal with it. I think we just accepted it as part of life and gave the girls advice on how to cope. I don't know of any incidents that would have actually amounted to assault, but if so we would have taken that much more seriously. I'd have left if there had been anything unpleasant.'

Deirdre Hyde
London

'I do remember being wary a lot of the time but never experienced anything serious. There were plenty of suggestions for meetings after work, lunchtime drinks, working late etc. which one kind of sensed had an ulterior motive and batted off without trying to cause offence or trouble. There was definitely casual sexual harassment of junior female employees in the form of unnecessary touching, invasion of private space, comments about one's clothing and appearance etc., often innuendo loaded; but that was endemic in society at that time.'

Amanda Lunt
London

'I guess at the BBC a new angle on the debs' acronym NSIT, "not safe in taxis" would have been NSIS, "not safe in studios"; but then you could exclude half the men on the BBC Rep who were batting for the other side.'

Wendy Gough
Midlands

'The chief officer had a plush office and you had to press a button if you wanted to get him to sign something, he never came upstairs. His PA was the head secretary as well as overseeing the other admin staff. He seemed nice, until at a Christmas dinner dance he ran his hand down my back (long dress with low back) and slipped his hand inside the back of my underwear. Loads of people saw, as we were at the bar. I was 18. I didn't say anything, just smiled and walked away. This was normal in those times. I wasn't particularly bothered, just avoided being in his office on my own from then on.'

Debbie Maya
London

'My boss stuck his tongue down my throat in the lift, after a lunch. I tried to push him off. He was pink, sweaty and ugly. I reported him and was told, "Oh don't worry, he was probably drunk".'

Patricia Delosrios
Not disclosed

'Horrible memories. A sweaty hand on you too long. Innuendos. Leaning over you. Peering at your breasts. So much went on. You couldn't complain if you wanted to keep your job.'

Christine Allsop
Chesterfield

'One secretary said the boss used to masturbate under the desk when he was dictating. Everyone knew it was true because that was the man he was. Nobody thought of complaining, we just thought, "What a w*nker". If you complained about anything the outcome was never good and it was not worth the effort. You just had to ignore it.'

A particularly shocking case emerged in 2014 in an interview with the late Baron Bell, the former public relations executive. In it he said, as Benét described, that in the advertising business female employees were regarded more as sex objects than equals. A good-looking secretary was a status symbol among managers, they would compete with each other to hire the most attractive one. Bell told the story of how a secretary attending a job interview had been informed that 'only' a woman with very large breasts would be appointed, and the interviewer asked her to remove her top and bra for inspection. Apparently she obliged, at which point other colleagues, including Tim Bell, were brought in to admire the sight. She got the job. At the time, he thought it was funny, but in the interview agreed it was disgusting and would now be considered unacceptable.[29]'

This was in an advertising company; somehow I doubt a job in a the Civil Service or at a branch of the local bank would have had the same entry requirements, and plenty of women would have walked out of the room had they been asked to perform in this way.

Helen Gurley Brown was adamant that there was no such thing as an innocent victim. 'Girls' she wrote, weren't prey, they were capable of standing up for themselves and saying "No" when necessary.[30] Some contributors too were keen to make this point too.

Sarah Oram
London

'I did confront people. On one occasion somebody was a little over the top, so I walloped him. He was so surprised he didn't quite know what had hit him, I don't think he had had that happen before. I had forgotten that what I'd got in my hand was the very heavy phone book.

'There was another very persistent, very annoying person, and another friend had brought in some bedding because they were moving flats. So another secretary and I made a bed up somewhere and invited him in, calling his bluff. I suppose we were very lucky because he ran a mile. We never had a problem with him again.'

Sue MacCulloch
London

'There were four of us secretaries in the one room. If anyone came in and bothered us there were the other three, and if he did try it on we would just stare at him. We had medical reps who thought they could chance their arm, but they were just frozen out, I'm afraid, if they fell foul of us. I never felt threatened or unsafe. We had dividing lines between what was and wasn't funny.'

Amanda Lunt
London

'Sexual harassment became much more apparent when I was working in a non-secretarial role in television studios, and in this respect the climate between radio and television (with the possible exception of the popular music stations) seemed to be different. There was some sexual innuendo, but most of it was fairly harmless banter which one tolerated as it helped to oil the wheels and lightened the working day.

'There was one incident in which a very attractive girl, a few years younger than me, in the most junior studio role, was being constantly harassed by one of the more senior studio staff who had the power to report on her progress and thus affect her career. Representations to management were of no avail (the prevailing attitude seeming to be that if you couldn't stand the heat, you should get out of the kitchen) and I suspect some of the all-male managers would have secretly enjoyed the chance to get more closely acquainted with her themselves. Eventually I persuaded her to join the staff union, who took up the case and the culprit, though not dismissed, was severely reprimanded and steps taken to ensure they were no longer scheduled to work together.'

Olwen Hanson
Yorkshire

'During my induction, when attending the sales reps' meeting, I was the only female and was teased by one rep that I had chosen to sit next to the oldest man. So I promptly moved to sit next to him and asked if he was happy with that. He was extremely embarrassed, much to the delight of the rest of the team. We got on fine after that.'

Jan Jones
Manchester

'One boss was able to get a discount on things like carpets, so when I moved into a new flat I asked for his help. He said, "Fine", but wanted a key to my flat to have little afternoon liaisons there! Obviously, I said, "No". But I used to find, along with the rest of the girls, that having a damn good laugh at their expense, which they knew we did, was a pretty good cure.'

Lesley Powell
Not disclosed

'There was a smarmy man who used to make comments of a sexual nature when I went in to his office and this made me feel very uncomfortable. I confided in a friend who advised me to ask him to refrain. The next time he was having a meeting with two colleagues from other offices, I took in the coffee, and he said "Here comes our sex queen". I was shaking inside but I summoned all my courage and said something like "Mr …. , please will you not make such remarks". Nobody said a word, but I think because his colleagues were there and they were decent people it did the trick. He never did it again.'

Susan Coles
London

'I worked for an agency that managed pop stars. This job had a large turnover of female staff, here today, gone tomorrow. When I joined there were two attractive girls working as hostesses, and then I just didn't see them any more. I did my job as required, but eventually I was given short notice to leave because, to quote, "I did not have the Bunny Girl image!" I had already met another girl who was being shown around, I am sure she was lined up to take my place.

'This dismissal came out of the blue, I was not warned nor handed a letter. I think it was just a case of my face not fitting anymore, or perhaps wanting to give a friend the job. My parting shot was that I could say a lot (e.g. my boss trying to seduce me) but I would not waste my breath. I have to say I cried all the way home because I was so shocked at being treated like that. I complained, and was given compensation of two months' pay.

'I then went from the frying pan into the fire, as I answered an ad to work for a very upper class, married man in his home in Lord North Street in London. This job was a disaster as the man was a sleaze. Part of my job was to drive him around, I'm not sure if he had lost his licence. I drove him to Newmarket once to the races and he bought me lunch. Perhaps I allowed him to become too familiar in this way; however, I had many lunches with other bosses without being propositioned.

'I cannot remember why or how I left on the day I did, but I clearly had concerns about this man's behaviour. I used to go out to one of those little photocopying places and I remember asking the man there if many girls working for this man came and went, and he told me they did. That led me to believe that he had behaved inappropriately with others and was my cue to go too. I took my P45 and never returned.'

Jan Jones
Manchester

'I got involved in the annual conferences, and one year we took the show "on the road" to Glasgow and London. I remember London particularly, because my boss took me to the London Palladium; ironically I think it was to see *No Sex Please, We're British*. As we sat there, I became aware of an arm creeping across the back of my seat. He offered me a lift home and when we got back to the hotel he wanted a kiss. I slapped him across the face. No one has ever got out of a taxi as fast as I did. Luckily he didn't know my room number. The next day I mentioned the event to one of the conference crew who I knew quite well, and he acted as a bit of a barrier.

'On the trip home, my boss got quite drunk but insisted on driving me back, as often happened in those days with no drink-driving ban. When we got there, my flatmate was home and he then pursued her (not altogether unwillingly on her part it has to be said). I can't remember how I eventually got him out of the flat.

'The next day, I couldn't wait to get in to tell the girls in the office all about this. He was late coming in and rang me at the office, not to apologise but to ask me not to tell the others. Obviously I said I wouldn't, but by then they already knew. It was never mentioned again and thankfully he left the company not that long after.'

Sarah Oram
London

'There was a secretary, well-liked: he was a senior marketing guy, intensely disliked. He wasn't often at our after-work socialising with the tech guys and sociable sales force, so I guess he was not that liked by them either. He was a self-important little man, a very distinct type. I'm sure you've met them as well.

'Anyway, she got in a taxi with this guy, I'm not sure how she ended up with him but they may have been the last two on board at the end of an evening. Whatever he did, she fended him off and got out of the taxi. Had she not been able to react, and she wasn't a shrinking violet, it would have been something far more serious. It was definitely an attack. I can't remember any follow on, in those days they would have taken his side and not hers.'

Although nearly all of those who wrote to me were glad sexual harassment had been identified, and welcomed the progress made since the 1970s, there was also a sense that perhaps something had been lost too.

Judith Farnell
Yorkshire

'I'm glad I worked when I did, when my male bosses felt OK about putting an arm round you if you were upset or touching your hand to show sympathy. I was very quiet and shy as a young woman but I could stand up for myself and never felt threatened. I think women nowadays are pathetic — they always want someone else to stand up for them and if someone says the slightest thing that could be construed as an insult they take it that way and run home to mummy. Yet at the same time they say they are strong and feminist! Rubbish — they're weak and unassertive. They need to get a backbone and get a grip and not allow men to be disrespectful. I'm sick to the back teeth of virtue signalling authors.'

Hazel Channon
Not disclosed

'In the modern day too much emphasis is given to sexual harassment by the press. I am told by males that they cannot even comment on how well dressed a colleague might be! Ridiculous!'

Amanda Lunt
London

'I have to admit to feeling that the pendulum has swung a bit too far in the other direction, and imagine those in any sphere of working life now have to be much more aware of even mild flirtation and the kind of harmless banter which we indulged in, even if it helped to bond a team together and lighten the mood. Given that a large proportion of the population are said to meet their future partner at work, if they have to tread so cautiously in initiating a relationship, one fears for the future of the human race.'

Deirdre Hyde
London

'A lot is written and said about these matters nowadays e.g. #metoo, but I am not sure it will change things overmuch for "ordinary" women. Those attitudes still exist, particularly towards those in what are still regarded as subordinate positions. Having said that, there are plenty of women who enjoy the attention.'

Olwen Hanson
Yorkshire

'It is encouraging to know that discrimination, bullying, harassment etc. are now dealt with more robustly – although I have to say that I think that some gentle teasing between people who know each other well should be treated as such.'

*****

The myth of the sexy secretary persists, even today. As recently as 2013, Channel 4 broadcast a series of TV programmes of which one episode looked at the 'changing face of British offices through the relationship between bosses and their secretaries'. The title of this episode, *Confessions of a Secretary*, is a bit of a clue as to the angle it took. As well as the Tim Bell story mentioned previously, the programme included an interview with Jacquee Storozynski-Toll, who described various incidents, including one in which her boss had put her across his knee and spanked her in full view of her colleagues. What was particularly shocking was that none of them saw nothing unusual in this. On another occasion a senior manager put his hand up her skirt while she made a phone call[31].

I wanted to know more, and contacted Jacquee. I was surprised to learn that she, and the other women who appeared in the programme with similar stories, had in fact never been secretaries. They were working in other roles, in her case as a journalist, and may have become the targets of sexual harassment because they were breaking into areas of employment which had traditionally been exclusively male, possibly even being tested with initiation rites. What this episode tells us is that even now there is media mileage in depicting secretaries as the victims of, or even willing participants in, sexual harassment, irrespective of its actual prevalence.

So I hope this chapter has helped to adjust perceptions, to set the record straight. Attitudes towards women in the workplace have changed so much since the 1970s that it seems almost bizarre today that secretaries were seen as dim but flirty office accessories, to be used by men to score points off each other or be manipulated by management; and that women who complained about being treated offensively or humiliated were told to shut up and go away. However, we should remember that plenty of women, despite an absence of support from their superiors or from the law, stood up for themselves, supported each other and made it clear what was acceptable behaviour. I'd suggest that much depended on the culture of each office, and that Margaret Knowles was close to the truth when she said, 'I think men knew whether they could or could not'.

It would be wrong too to assume that, simply because of the close attention paid to the seamier side of the 70s, these were the worst years of mistreatment and misogyny at work — both existed long before then and continue to the present day. What was unique to the decade was its emphasis on youth, freedom and a relaxing of standards of behaviour, all of which became embodied in the image of the dolly bird/secretary. Both she and the office wife tell us more about male expectations than they do about the women whom they were supposed to represent; so much so that at the time I never connected either image to the people I knew in the real world and assumed no one else did either.

Why does this matter now? Because the ubiquity of both images closed down alternative ways of thinking about secretaries, they *could only* be patient and deferential office wives, or chirpy but dim dollies. As a result, there was no need to take secretaries seriously, to address issues of inequality or offensive behaviour towards them. The images demeaned the women on to whom they were projected and trivialised the value of their work. So let's consign the office wife and the sexy secretary to a bin marked 'Male Fantasies,' shut the lid and leave them there. Instead, we'll celebrate the achievements of the real women instead — in the next chapter.

Chapter 6 : The secretarial trap

In 1976, Frances Cairncross[32], economist and academic, wrote an article in *The Guardian* headlined 'The Secretary Bird Trap' in which she warned any current school or college-leavers who were thinking of becoming secretaries that 99 times out of a 100 the job was a dead end. It would lead only to a lifetime of tedious and uninteresting work. Secretaries, as she put it, were 'writhing in frustration'. Nor was marriage a reliable means of escape. A secretary might, by choice or through lack of a suitable partner, remain single; if married, she might be divorced or widowed. In such cases she would need a reliable source of income for the rest of her life, so how much better it would be to seek a more rewarding career from the outset. The final words of advice in her article were that, whatever readers did, they should avoid learning shorthand and typing[33].

Once upon a time, secretarial work had been a source of liberation for women from dependence on their families: now it had become a trap. What had happened?

Feminist writers were already pushing against the straitjacket of assuming women would only be capable of performing supportive roles at work. Germaine Greer, in *The Female Eunuch* published in 1970, observed that the qualities traditionally associated with the 'feminine:' modesty, obedience, anxiety to please, were those associated with underdogs or eunuchs — also, we note, the office wife. Working women had to make a choice between being successful or being ' nice'. As far as secretaries were concerned, Mary Kathleen Bénet explored this further. She claimed it was this willingness to deny themselves ambition that made women so employable as secretaries. A boss would never appoint a male one because he wouldn't want the competition; but a woman bolstered his ego by being deferential and allowing him to think that, however good she was at her job, he was even better at his.

The motivation for Cairncross's article was the growing demand for better opportunities for women; bear in mind that it wasn't until the middle of the decade that the Equal Opportunities Commission even began its work. The post-war generation of women had, on the whole, been better educated and had greater expectations of what they might achieve than those which had gone before. However, was she right to represent secretarial work as a dead end job, and to advise girls against taking it on?

I read *The Female Eunuch* when it first appeared and I have to say I found it completely baffling. I couldn't relate Greer's portrayal of men to any that I had met, and her emphasis on sex, given that I had zilch experience of it at the time, was even more puzzling. In fact, the views expressed in the book seemed so extreme to me that I remained ambivalent about, even suspicious of, feminism for the rest of the decade. Had others felt the same?

Sharon Tagle
Philadelphia

'I was aware [of feminism]. That's when I joined a group that had just formed, WAJE (Women's Alliance for Job Equity). It was pretty exciting to be at the forefront of this movement in Philadelphia. Our motto was "Raises, Not Roses." One year we held a Most Demeaning Secretarial Task contest, won by a woman who had been asked to sew up her boss's pants while he was still in them.'

Alison Chubb
London

'I read *The Feminine Mystique* and *The Female Eunuch* around the time that I worked as a temp. They weren't so much a revelation as a confirmation of views I had already formed and they made me feel I was not alone.'

Anne Ballard
Toronto/London

'I became an ardent feminist during my years as a secretary. In Canada, apart from being bored, my only complaint was when I found the male office junior, aged 18, earned more than I did, because he was "a man with a family."'

Elaine Day
London

'I don't specifically remember the secretarial role being written about, but I was very influenced by Germaine Greer and *The Female Eunuch* and read other feminist writers at the time.'

Deirdre Hyde
London

'I was totally unaware of what was being written about secretaries by feminist writers at the time. I think I just accepted the status quo and didn't question it. Women's Rights groups? I confess I was not aware of their existence or attitudes.'

You might have imagined contributors would have supported Greer, Benét and Cairncross for bringing the limitations of their job to public attention but, with the exception the four people quoted above, the majority said they hadn't been aware of feminism in the 70s and a few added that they didn't agree with it either. Most were content to accept that theirs had been a supportive role and saw nothing frustrating or demeaning about having performed it.

Why is this? Perhaps partly because the feminist argument, which was still very new in the 70s, was turning on its head the culture in which they had been brought up. At the time, it seemed perfectly normal that bosses were (mostly) men and secretaries (mostly) women. But more importantly, perhaps, it was because feminists tended to make the same mistakes as everyone else did when writing about secretaries. Like Greer, they assumed that they were dutiful office wives or, like Benét, sexy dolly birds. To some extent this is understandable because hard evidence about what secretaries actually did all day was lacking — Silverstone's doctorate research, for example, wasn't published. The problem was that few men were typists and few women were bosses but, in attacking the role as a prime example of the gender inequality, feminists forgot to support the women who performed it and the value of their work. *Someone* had to type all those letters and answer the phone and, given the technology of the time, secretaries saved their employers huge amounts of time and money by being those who did it. And as far as secretaries themselves were concerned, being told by women who knew little about them that they lacked the wit or willpower to escape a perceived trap left them feeling shot in the back by their sisters.

Amanda Lunt
London

'I felt that secretaries were an easy target. Generally we performed a useful function (with hindsight, fulfilling many of the tasks now performed by current technology) and anyone who was in a job in which they felt demeaned or ill-treated had the means to find themselves something else.'

Lucy Fisher
London

'Aaaaactuallleeee ... it just meant that they despised secretaries. Nobody was "a secretary,", they were "just a secretary", like being "just a housewife". People used to be shocked when I told them I was a secretary.'

A suspicion of female academics may have also arisen because, while most of the graduates who became secretaries were capable, there were always a few who were determined to show that they felt the job was beneath them. They yawned, stared out of the window, complained about having to do 'all this' typing, undid a few blouse buttons for an unimpressed (and possibly terrified) boss and left others to complete their work so it caught the post. Complaints about a lack of promotion from them fell on very deaf ears. What was the use of a degree in Eng Lit, if you couldn't, or wouldn't on principle, produce a decent business letter?

Tanya Bruce Lockhart
London

'The graduates I interviewed [for jobs at LWT] didn't really want to get their hands dirty. They weren't good at going to chat up the chippies or being nice to the sparks or being good with other people. They thought they had a degree and they were there to do a specific task. They weren't flexible.'

Cairncross's description of the secretarial trap prompted a couple replies. The first was from a Mrs Goodhew of Pinner. In her experience, she said, secretarial work meant being wholly dependent on someone else's thoughts, plans and workflow. She had been incensed at having commas and full stops dictated to her and signed up to study for a degree in English, hoping it would lead her to work in a different capacity. It didn't. So yes, she agreed there was a trap. (Perhaps Mrs Goodhew wasn't aware that bosses often dictated the punctuation marks when they wanted to work out what to say next, and the punctuation marks were usually wrong anyway.) The second letter, from Peter Pitman of Pitmans Training Services, reminded readers that learning secretarial skills was useful for girls for whom a professional career was out of reach. It virtually guaranteed them a job too; in Central London there were six vacancies for every available secretarial worker.[34]. (Whatever the truth of this, you might consider he had a vested interest.)

Further evidence supporting the secretarial trap comes from Rosalie Silverstone, who found that only 5 per cent of her secretaries felt certain of a chance of promotion, as opposed to the 58 per cent who believed they had none. What these women wanted, as much as better pay and status, was greater responsibility. Silverstone quoted one as saying,

> 'I thought a secretarial course would provide a "stepping stone" to other jobs. In the majority of cases this just doesn't work. One gets in a rut and apathy sets in. We are often regarded as being thick. The main problem is that one never does original, thought-provoking work, one only handles another's thoughts. It's all very frustrating.'.[35]

*****

So were all secretaries caught in a trap? It came down to a vicious circle. The trap most young women feared wasn't that of getting stuck behind a typewriter; it was of becoming a spinster. They would have known 'maiden' aunts and neighbours who had lost sweethearts during the war, or 'never met Mr Right', women whose achievements were always tinged with pity for their single status. So, in the absence of any established route out of the secretarial role, and rather than push against a very strong tide of expectation with a risk of being mocked by friends and family, it was simpler to put their effort into finding husbands, with the result that women weren't promoted because managers thought they would leave: women left because they weren't promoted.

Ann Ballard
London

'It was absolutely true that secretarial work was a trap. Of course in some places, like firms of solicitors for instance, you clearly needed to be qualified to succeed, but in others it would have been commonsense to promote capable women. Instead, while we carried on typing, we saw clueless young men with degrees being brought in to do work we could have done better. Why? Sexism, elitism, lack of imagination. To be fair, they had such difficulty in finding good secretaries that they were probably terrified of losing us.'

Elaine Day
London

'The prevailing attitude in the 1970s was still that women were likely to get married and have a family, so what's the point of educating them or offering them unrealistic career expectations? I can remember being very shocked when a friend of my parents' said this about his three daughters – in fact they went on to higher education and good jobs in spite of his attitude!'

Mary Ankrett
Walsall

'Most bosses felt that secretaries were satisfied with that role and anyway, there was no opportunity in most companies for a secretary to be anything other than a secretary. I worked as PA to a Chairman and Managing Director of a contract caterer and recruited all the office staff. The directors decided to appoint a personnel manager to recruit some categories of catering staff. I told my boss I would like to apply for it. He said, "You've got a job, and what do you know about recruiting?" To which I replied, "I am already doing it for the office staff." He passed over that and said, "Come on, we've got work to do, shall we get on with it?"

Christine Allsop
Chesterfield

'I definitely [felt] trapped. You were really a paid skivvy for men who had no idea what they were doing. I tried a couple of times to better myself but was always shot down in flames. Nobody escaped unless they got pregnant.'

When Silverstone questioned employers about what opportunities were available for secretaries within their firms she received responses like these:

'Women just don't get on in the business world, but if you want to try, becoming a secretary is one of the worst ways to begin.'

''I doubt whether working in an office ... is a training for learning a business. You would need to meet lots of people and attend courses. In this firm you could go to Head Office if you were very bright, where two of the divisional managers have more PA-type jobs and secretaries travel around with them, but that's about all.'

''Once a secretary, always a secretary. I made one exception and tried it, and she had spent so many years doing what other people wanted that she could not think for herself.'

In 1971 Ralph Cooper, training manager at Pye Business Communications Ltd in Royston, Hertfordshire, introduced a positive discrimination scheme called 'Female Career Development'. Its aim was to improve the status of their office 'girls', some of whom had university degrees. Cooper wanted to promote them into junior executive vacancies that had previously been occupied by a manager with a secretary. According to an article in *The Guardian*, two former secretaries became managers of the transport fleet and maintenance services, while another was put in charge of the marketing department's 'secretarial services', which sounds suspiciously like a typing pool. The article quotes one of the maintenance engineers as saying with surprised delight, 'It's no different from working for a man!' What happened to this scheme and the women Cooper promoted I have been unable to discover, but the fact that it made the national press shows how revolutionary an idea it was[36].

The standard method of dealing with an employment grievance in the 1970s was to form or join a trade union and, if necessary, take industrial action, but secretaries didn't do this, at least, not in the UK. Being of a more traditional frame of mind, and with loyalty to their boss uppermost in their minds, they simply offloaded onto other members of the mafia or changed job. Not so in the United States, where secretaries were a lot more feisty and proactive. They formed groups, such as '9to5' in Boston and took direct action. They refused to serve coffee to their bosses, the task which they felt most typified their 'feminine' role. The result was they were fired. Back in the UK, editor of *The Guardian*'s women's page, Mary Stott, offered them support and observed that the men might actually benefit from making their own coffee, a few minutes away from the desk would give them time to think[37].

As Anne Ballard explained, in areas where professional or scientific qualifications were essential for promotion, secretarial skills alone would only get you into an administrative post. However, in business or the arts there was a better chance of making progress. Silverstone recommended secretaries to take a course in business studies, although as mature students this might have been difficult to manage. She also recommended companies should set up internal career structures so secretaries could be promoted into other areas of work. The BBC was one employer already doing this, as it opened its internal vacancies to all applicants. However, there was a problem: competition for positions was intense.

Denise Tomlinson
London

'I became acting researcher/assistant producer at the end of my time at BBC TV. It wasn't so much that secretarial skills and experience typecast me, so much as my lack of a degree. And I didn't have what the head of department called "fire in my belly". I got fed up with the constant having to compete for opportunities. The permanent jobs always seemed to go to newcomers with Oxbridge degrees and no experience. With hindsight I probably would have tried to get more qualifications, but at the time it wasn't possible.'

Debbie Maya
London

'In the BBC, graduates had many doors opened to them to apply for studio management jobs, vision mixing, production jobs, etc. They favoured public school and Oxbridge grads.'

Valerie Docker
London

'At the BBC, when I first asked about promotion they just said, "No, you haven't got a degree," not, "We think you are bright enough to do some things". Then I asked, "Could I do research?" because I had started Open University studies and was getting on well with them. I said, "I don't really like the secretarial role and I would be more interested in production". I remember this Personnel lady just saying, "No", and waving her hand across the desk, just like that: "No". Eventually, they did send me on a production course and I was told, "Yes, we'll start you off, there's a place in Reading you can go to". Well, of course being a young lass in London I didn't want to go to Reading, to me it felt like two or three hours away.'

*****

For myself, it was a gradual process over a couple of years before I realised I had become trapped. While at the BBC, my boss advised me that to get any further I would need a university degree, so I re-took an A-level at an evening class and was offered places conditional on the result. Unfortunately, just before the exam a family bereavement derailed that plan completely, so I left the Corporation to join William Kimber, thinking that at a smaller firm I would have a better chance of moving from secretarial to more creative work.

Although the job was interesting to begin with, I realised fairly soon this wasn't going to happen because Mr Kimber didn't need two editors and no receptionist. The next logical step would have been to apply for a PA job somewhere else in publishing, but I didn't want to have to dress in suits and heels and, as I imagined it, simper like an office wife. For me, coffee came in a mug, not bone china. Also, I didn't understand business. I couldn't see why, when all I needed was enough money to pay for meals and the rent, companies were so focussed on making bigger and bigger profits. And I definitely didn't want a job that would be stressful or demand late evenings at work.

So by the time Cairncross's article was published I had become stuck, but nonetheless had found a sort of solution. Having read *Down and Out in Paris and London*, I had reinvented myself as George Orwell, only with less tweed and tobacco. I had left Kimbers and, somewhat presciently, imagining myself as an undercover reporter, had become a 'temp', a temporary secretary. In this guise I roamed the offices of the City and West London, sliding anonymously from place to place while collecting information about their operations. I'll tell you more about that in the next chapter, but the results of my research, if you're interested, were that all offices were staffed by the same sort of people, and all you needed to know on Day One was (a) whether your boss was organised or away with the fairies, (b) who were the ones who did all the work (usually the secretaries and/or junior managers) and (c) what were the arrangements for lunch.

Actually, to be totally honest, I think that the real reason behind my decision to become a temp was less about the sleuthing than a need to widen the field of potential boyfriends en route to finding a husband, a strategy which paid off eventually. At a security company in Hounslow, where the redoubtable Rita forged documents so that clients never found out their contracts hadn't been fulfilled and a friendly salesman bought me lunch, disguising me on his expenses form as British Road Parcels Ltd, I met my future husband.

*****

So, secretaries were all trapped by societal expectations into dead-end jobs. Was this so? Well, we can find a glimmer of hope in Silverstone's research. As well as those negative views from employers we saw earlier, she found some that were more positive.

> 'It must be a good beginning, because it is useful to know how things work. They get to know how things function from the beginning — it's like a man being on the shop floor and becoming the Managing Director.'

> 'It must be a good training because it allows a person to get an insight into the top executive's world without the responsibility.[38]'

So how could a secretary escape? Looking at contributors' accounts, it seems to me there were several useful tools, each of which was insufficient on its own but, when used in combination, could become very effective.

The first was simply acquiring credit for doing the existing job well. The difficulty here was that efficiency is more evident in its absence than presence but without having built up a good reputation as a reliable worker promotion was a non-starter. Hence, the bored graduate secretaries. Being good at your job wasn't enough, you had to be *noticed* for it too. Gurley Brown had some ideas about this which were decidedly non-feminist. Men, she said, were not the obstacle to a secretary's ambitions, they simply didn't like career-minded women who hated men.[39] She recommended secretaries should deploy 'typical' feminine wiles, devoting a whole chapter to make-up and clothes. This included a recommendation which only those who were really serious about going places would be likely to adopt, viz, eating lots of fresh liver so you looked beautiful and healthy. About a pound a week should do the trick. Assuming this brought you to everyone's attention and you weren't poisoned by Vitamin A, she advised reading trade journals, buttering up the bosses and fixing a heart-to-heart talk to ask for a specific job, presumably wearing one of those unbuttoned blouses[40].

It was certainly a good idea to work for a boss who supported your ambitions, rather than one who was desperate to prevent you leaving, and to get him on your side.

Tanya Bruce Lockhart
London Weekend Television

'Frank [Muir] was very good, he used to let me read scripts and comment on them, and that was my springboard to becoming a producer because I knew how to edit.

'One of the big, major series we did while I was still a secretary was *The Complete and Utter History of Britain,* which was the Battle of Hastings and all that. In it were Terry Jones and Michael Palin who subsequently did *Monty Python.* I used to go on location to places all over England. We were always looking for classical backdrops or castles and I went everywhere, amazingly, with the dog and the camera crew. I organised all these people, their food and where they were staying. It was good fun.'

In fact, many bosses did encourage their secretaries' ambitions.

Sonia Lovett
BBC

'After becoming a television production assistant and then a vision mixer, I went on to direct, specialising in music programmes and opera in particular. When I started working as a production assistant for Rodney Greenberg in the [BBC's] Music and Arts Department, he was happy to let me direct and vision-mix one of the Elisabeth

Schwarzkopf master classes recorded at the Edinburgh Festival. It was very generous of him.

'Humphrey Burton was also very helpful. I sat with him for days while he scripted operas and he often asked for my opinion on the camera script. On one occasion I directed and vision-mixed the first camera rehearsal of *Eugene Onegin* because he had a prior engagement that day. It was so much more enjoyable for me to feel I was contributing.

'Becoming a BBC secretary opened the door to many opportunities for me.'

Qualifications were handy, but often needed to be combined with appropriate experience before they became a valuable tool.

Amanda Lunt
BBC

'Initially, a degree might have helped with confidence and in gaining promotion, but in the end I don't think it made much difference. The few graduate secretaries I knew didn't progress much further up the ladder than I did. Some left altogether out of frustration or boredom.

'It was the graduates who came to the BBC a little later in life, with experience and skills in other areas (such as theatre, law, education and so on) who had the edge.'

Membership of professional organisations, such as the IQPS (Institute of Qualified Private Secretaries) or the EAPS (European Association of Professional Secretaries), was useful because they provided advice, support and opportunities for networking.

Mary Ankrett
Walsall

'In my time with EAPS, I became their regional co-ordinator and part of my role was to organise the annual UK conference. One of my guest speakers was a man named Graham Day, who was the boss of the Austin Rover Group. In his talk at the conference he said, "During your life you need a basketfull of skills. Sometimes, at the time you are gaining them, you may not think they are useful, but later on in life there suddenly becomes a need for them. It is, therefore, a good idea to make a plan to have a basket full of skills on which you can call. Never turn down an opportunity to learn something new." I have never forgotten that.'

As we saw in the first chapter, the training offered to British secretaries was generally of a lower standard than that in other countries. It equipped them for the job itself but little more, so what further training might there be?

Lorraine Oliver
Guinness Brewery, Park Royal, London

'It's always useful to obtain further knowledge. I went for a job in the brewery in a department dealing with Europe. I was asked if I spoke French and German. I said I had French O-level but I'd never learnt German at school, was asked if I'd be willing to learn and ended up agreeing to German evening classes, which I did for five years. When my boss was abroad I had to go to the Linguaphone room and practise German. I did lots of training in all jobs: first aid, various machines and so on.'

Olwen Hanson
Engineering, Yorkshire

'The company was keen to offer training opportunities and I took advantage of these, so another part of my role became to interview staff for clerical positions at the six sales offices throughout the north-west. My first interviews entailed an overnight hotel stay (scary thought) in Kendal, followed a couple of years later by flying to Belfast (even more scary, especially as the hotel I had stayed in was bombed about a month later).

'In other jobs, training resulted in former secretaries being promoted to personnel officer, overseas representative and head of finance. There were better opportunities in large companies. Even when handing in my notice at the insurance company I was asked to reconsider and offered training for a senior role in the finance department, definitely NOT for me!

'The secretarial trap was certainly prevalent when I started work in the mid-1960s but has definitely changed over the years. With my third job, there were more opportunities for advancement and I know of several secretaries in that company who went on to managerial roles. This change was probably led by large companies where more opportunities were available.'

One method of training at the BBC was the system of attachments. A member of staff was given a temporary attachment for a stipulated period, say six months, moving from one department to another. This gave both parties the opportunity to try each other out, and was great for the licence payers because the attached person was paid at the old, and usually lower, rate. Some people went from one attachment to another for years.

Amanda Lunt
BBC, London

'I made two escape attempts, both via the BBC's excellent attachment scheme. The first was quite competitive, a welcome break from the typewriter as an Assistant Floor Manager in television, roughly equivalent to an ASM in the theatre, helping to run rehearsals for children's and comedy programmes, prompting artists and being in charge of studio or filming props. I had equipped myself for it by talking to people who had done the job (largely via the BBC Club social network), lurking around TV studios at weekends and working backstage on amateur productions. I enjoyed it and found I had useful practical skills for things like making props for *Play School* out of cereal packets and egg boxes. But the long studio working days, mostly on your feet, were pretty tiring. I decided that I didn't really want to pursue a career for which I probably didn't possess sufficient physical stamina.

'After a few years in Radio Drama I decided to move on again. Initially, I applied for a training attachment to Personnel, something to which I felt I might be well suited after several years as a staff union representative. I was somewhat mystified not even to be offered a preliminary interview. My personnel officer made the surprising admission that I might find myself frustrated in a climate where Personnel were required to do the bidding of management, and more or less implied that my union activities (which could hardly be construed as militant) might not have endeared me to them.

'Realising I'd had a lucky escape, soon afterwards I applied for another attachment, this time to the Programme Contracts department, which engaged artists for radio drama and elsewhere, a post for which my production experience had laid a lot of the groundwork. Within six months it turned into a permanent job and I acquired my own secretary.

'The other day I remembered a phrase which appeared more than once in my earlier BBC annual reports (works of art in themselves at times) which mentioned that I was "very willing". It's not something anyone would dare to use now, which just goes to show how times have changed. I guess it was either damning with faint praise, and/or implied that one was prepared to muck in and help out generally without complaint.'

But further training for secretaries wasn't always on offer.

Christine Allsop
Engineering, Chesterfield

'I was working as secretary to the Works Manager of a large, well-known engineering firm. I noticed that there was no one at the time doing the Human Resources side of the business, it was just done on an ad hoc basis by anyone and this was not very efficient or professional. I found a suitable course which could be done at a local college and asked if I could take it. The Works Manager shouted at me, told me off for even asking and said there was no way this was going to happen. I was made to feel really bad for even thinking about it.'

So far, the escape weapon kit includes: efficiency, getting attention, encouragement from the boss, qualifications, membership of a professional body and training. But the biggest bazooka in the bunch was something that was never mentioned at college or in the handbooks: the ability to spot an opportunity and the determination to make the most of it. This wasn't always easy. Because a secretary worked closely with one boss, it was often difficult for her to grasp the wider picture of the company or the business, and to be identify potential opportunities for her. Hers was a parochial view, one that would be quickly exposed at an interview. The answer was to learn everything she could about the business, and go for it.

Elaine Day
BBC, London

'I volunteered for everything going! You couldn't just sit back and wait for it to be offered, you had to go out and grab it.'

Gwen Rhys
London

'I wasn't trapped, I got a lot of promotion early on. I always wanted to run my own business and that was what I did in 1979, when I was 26. It wasn't called running a business then, it was called "working for yourself".

'I ran a word-processing bureau. I built it up, and had three full time staff and a couple of part-timers. By the mid-1980s I had introduced remote working. When one of my team moved to Kent, I purchased a PC for her to use at home, she paid me back over two years. I used to send her transcription work in the post, she would send me back a disc and the audio tapes. I had a laser printer (it cost me a LOT of money, thousands if I recall rightly) but it gave me a competitive edge. My team could key in all day and we spooled the work to print out all night. Fast, very accurate turnaround.

'I remember Sophie Mirman, who started Sock Shop (or whatever it was called) had been PA to either the MD or

Chairman of Marks and Spencer. She used his network of connections to tap into.'

Gwen's use of women working from home was an innovation perhaps few male employers would have considered.

Mary Ankrett
Walsall

'Although I loved my job, when I was passed over for the recruitment post I felt the need for a challenge, not a secretarial role. No training was ever offered to me, any I did was of my own volition. Whilst doing my LCCI (London Chamber of Commerce and Industry) Executive Secretary's Diploma I had studied management techniques etc., which had given me a thirst for something different. I had a wealth of knowledge of running a business, so I enrolled on a management course, after which I decided to start my own. At one point in my early career, I had taken a teacher's diploma to teach secretarial subjects so I decided to start a training centre for IT, typewriting, shorthand and book-keeping. I set it all up and became an RSA examination centre.'

Lucy Fisher
London

'At Thames and Hudson I thought they'd notice my brilliance and promote me to editor within a few weeks. They didn't. They just noticed my terrible typing and bolshy attitude.

'I was looking through the ads in one of those free magazines as usual, and I noticed that "Word Processor Operators" earned £7,000 a year. A secretary in publishing earned £5,000 — publishers expected their staff to be living rent-free in a flat bought by Daddy, my father wanted us all to stand on our own feet.

'So I thought "bugger publishing" and did a word-processing course. Then I was hired for a week (using an actual computer) as a temp at the *Financial Times* newsletters, got offered the job at the end of the week and spent the next seven years there as an Editorial Production Assistant. This may have been due to my being a bit of a bimbo. When that all came to an end, I applied for a subeditor's job on a computer magazine, did a subbing test, got the job and the rest is history.'

Anne Ballard
London

'I found legal work interesting and I picked it up quickly. Also, the people (not all men) I worked for seemed of mixed ability, and I thought myself at least as intelligent as they were. The idea of qualifying as a solicitor crept up on me when I learned that I could do so without a degree through an apprenticeship, and then that if I did a couple of A-levels I could get a university place, which sounded like much more fun. Nobody particularly suggested it, but all the lawyers I told about the idea were encouraging. The last two firms I worked for employed me during college holidays and gave me excellent references. They proved to be my last experience of secretarial work. After university I became a solicitor, and never regretted it for a moment.'

Deirdre Hyde
London

'I didn't necessarily feel trapped as a secretary, but knew I wanted to do more. After a few years in a publishing job, a position was created in the company of Sales Promotion Manager and it became my new role. Instead of typing out press releases which had been dictated to me, I actually wrote them myself. Likewise, costings for display materials and press advertising, catalogues and the routine paraphernalia of a publicity department that I understood and of which I had plenty of experience.

'Salary increase was insignificant but the new status was terrific. I had a bigger office, shared with a copywriter. We used to do T*he Times* crossword most mornings. We photocopied it and stuck it on the pull-out tray-over-desk-drawer which we could close quickly if anyone came in. Also went to lots of meetings. Never volunteered to make coffee or tea or take minutes. I didn't get a secretary. One of my motivations was status. I wanted to say "I am a ...." rather than "I'm just a secretary".'

Sylvia Dale
Herts

'I had always regarded becoming a secretary as a means to an end. I thought I would welcome taking orders from someone else but I didn't. I hated shorthand, probably because I didn't care to take down someone else's thoughts. My boss hadn't shown much respect for my previous teaching career (apart from my grammatical knowledge) and later on, when we were looking through applications for an admin post, he said that I wouldn't have made the shortlist as teaching would have been irrelevant experience. I felt that teaching was useful experience for dealing with someone like him.

'I was very lucky as I was promoted into an admin grade because of the death of a colleague. I remained as secretary to the No 2 in the organisation for about another three years, but the extra work I did meant that other opportunities within the office opened up to me. Eventually I left secretarial work behind — hurray! In later years I used to keep quiet about my typing skills.'

Pam Robinson
Liverpool

'Littlewoods Mail Order division were taking on Correspondence Clerks and paying 30 per cent more than I was earning [as a secretary] so I applied and was taken on by them. This wasn't a secretarial job and I was there for three years and hated it most of the time. We had to clock in and clock out, very hierarchical structure and it just didn't suit me. That said, they trained me in training skills and I was promoted to Training Instructor, and they gave me day release to complete my OND, so it was worth hanging in there.

'So at age 20, I'd been promoted to the Training Department. This was around 1973/74 when the Equal Opportunities legislation was being introduced. Littlewoods Mail Order division was about 99 per cent female and they were obviously looking to tick boxes by encouraging women to advance within the organisation.

'I applied to the Civil Service and was successful. It was 1975 and the big plus, as well as other benefits, was working flexitime. I've often said that the three greatest inventions of the 20th century for women are the Pill, Lycra and flexitime!'

*****

If some secretaries were trapped and others scaled the escape ladder, a third group remains which we haven't yet considered:

those who were content to do the job. It may be that some were making the best of their situation — after all, they had to earn a living and, given the hurdles they might face and the stress of being rebuffed, who could blame them, but there were plenty who enjoyed the job and found it interesting and rewarding.

Sarah Oram
Computing. London

'I enjoyed being a secretary because I was good at it. I enjoyed solving problems. If you were setting up a filing system, you had to work out how someone would go looking for the information, and design it accordingly. I liked the challenge of having to deal with somebody's impossible writing. I used to get the awkward people who nobody else could deal with. You think, "Oh right, now I understand this person, I understand why he or she is behaving this way."

'I suppose we weren't very valued — I suspect in a lot of places the secretaries weren't valued at all, and of course they could be replaced. I never felt *unvalued* though, because I was appreciated for what I did. I suppose we weren't very valued — I suspect in a lot of places the secretaries weren't valued at all, and of course they could be replaced.'

Heather Pippins
Builders' merchants, Somerset

'The job was very interesting. It was the contact with all the different aspects of the company. I was talking to the actuaries, pension providers, property developers, all on a personal basis ... the liaison with branch managers and showroom managers.'

Mary L Cryns
Solicitors, Philadelphia

'I loved it when I was given the responsibility of setting up new cases without having to be told how it was done or what forms to fill out for various circumstances, who to call and when to set up the depositions. I had a big calendar at my desk and had to figure out when my attorney was free. I found this to be an accomplishment.

'I didn't feel trapped at all because I had a job that paid well. I was happy because I made more money than pretty much all my friends at that time. I was able to get my own apartment in San Francisco and live independently even by age twenty, which was fabulous. I was learning to do all kinds of stuff as a legal secretary because my attorney was teaching me and he wasn't as scary as I thought he would be. And I mainly loved to type and do transcription.'

Connie Nolan
Kent

'My mother started in the typing pool in the 1960s typing handwritten copy, then progressed to tapes in the 70s. She applied for promotion and was very proud to become secretary to the Chief Engineer in the 1980s using her shorthand. My mother saw it as career development.'

Phyllida Scrivens
London

'Job satisfaction came from a project completed well, going the extra mile to make my manager's job a little less stressful, meeting with his visitors and outside business colleagues and developing an excellent telephone manner.

As my confidence grew I could get far more out of the job. I never really felt trapped.'

Sue MacCulloch
London

'I get a bit sort of cross with views from feminists. If you went into secretarial work and just wanted to stay in secretarial work and it suited you, why should you not? If you went into secretarial work and wanted to go on a bit further into admin or whatever, the opportunity was there.'

Gill Bazovsky
London

'I didn't aspire to higher things other than being a secretary, I enjoyed my work. It really never seemed like a trap, perhaps because I wasn't trained for anything else. In those days being a secretary was a real job, which I did as best I could. Does that sound a bit feeble now?'

Although not an accurate survey, contributors' accounts suggest the numbers in the three groups of secretaries, those who felt trapped, those who didn't and those who went on to other things, were roughly equal, which isn't quite the same as saying 99 per cent out of 100 were stuck in a dead-end job. So what about Frances Cairncross's parting words of advice never to learn shorthand and typing? At this, contributors howled with both anger and laughter. Even if only a few still used shorthand, many emphasised how incredibly useful it had been to have learned to touch type. As one pointed out, it didn't automatically confine you to working as a typist, it was useful in other jobs, and invaluable when computers became standard in the office and home.

How far women's opportunities for employment have progressed since the 1970s is outside the scope of this book, but here is a little snapshot from a current office worker:

> 'There are low-level microagressions, like being expected to clear up after meetings when it's not your job, being expected to stay late or come in early to deal with someone else's event, having it be assumed you're not busy and someone else's to-do list is more urgent than yours when you're already swamped ... that a business manager is not the same as a receptionist, or a secretary, or a PA, and we all have our own important things we need to get done — not just make your coffee.
>
> 'I don't think I've actively been negatively impacted or my career limited by being a female office worker, but I've never been all that ambitious or career-focussed. The glass ceiling is real, and there's still a lot of work to do on that front to drive out casual misogyny as well as the actively malicious disregard of women in office work.
>
> 'On the other hand, I've been told a lot that if you get a job as a secretary in a good company when you're younger, it'll be easy to move up from there. There's a lot of room to grow in admin work, and it's entirely possible to find a niche and thrive in it and get promoted that way if you wanted to do that, but there's very much a feeling of "but why would you want to stay a secretary when you could go on to be a XYZ?" — like it's not enough to enjoy being a secretary for a career.'

Today, women are able to find employment in areas that would have been unthinkable to 70s' school leavers, but some old prejudices and assumptions remain. Cairncross was right to demand better employment opportunities for women and deserves thanks, along with others, for having campaigned for them. But to me it seems unfortunate that her zeal to improve careers for women, led her to exaggerate her case and presented an another inaccurate image of secretarial work.

Nevertheless, another group of people paid particular attention to what feminists were saying about the secretarial trap, and redeployed it for big profits. We will find out more about them in the last chapter, but until then here is a last word on the subject of ambition.

Claudia Vickers
Newcastle

'I kept a copy of *Great Expectations* in the drawer of my desk and read it when I was bored.'

Chapter 7 : The job carousel

In the 70s, a young man with a 'steady job' expected he would follow the same career all his working life; he might even achieve this by staying with the same employer. However, as we know, it was different for his secretary. If she needed a pay rise or wanted to leave a harassing boss she had little choice but to move on and, for those who were caught in the trap, a different pattern emerged: in the first six months, learn the job; next twelve months, enjoy doing it; last six months, get bored and apply for another job somewhere else. It all came together in another cyclical pattern: the job carousel.

The reason it was so much easier to move to another job was because of the enormous number of vacancies on offer. Silverstone, comparing the numbers of advertisements for secretaries in the Situations Vacant column for a specified day in the London *Evening Standard* in 1950 and 1970, found an increase from eight to 250[41]. In the 70s, *The Times* often had a whole page devoted to 'Women's Appointments,' of which the majority were secretarial or PA.

The information in the ads though, was often little help. Here is a typical one from *The Times* in 1974. Headed, 'Happy and helpful?' it appealed for an 'alert, efficient audio or shorthand PA/ Secretary with bags of initiative, a strong constitution and a sense of humour'. Any girl who could ensure that her boss went home as cheerful as he had arrived was 'to ring 491 3211 and ask for Janice'. You may notice the absence of hard information about what business this cheerful chap was involved in or at what level in his firm, still less any clue about the rate of pay. Secretaries had to learn to read between the lines of these ads when job hunting. Here are a few more examples:
"

'Attractive boss in young firm of Holborn solicitors requires capable secretary, £1,250 pa,'
How attractive, I wonder, and who decided he was — him?

'American oil company: working for senior international executives. Good speeds required, (electric typewriter).'
Ah, that electric typewriter was a major attraction, but it might indicate the job involved a lot of repetitive typing.

'Total absorption in the affairs of a Director of a Merchant Bank offered to mature secretary between 28 and 45; over £2,000 pa with LVs,'
A PA's job and, unlike today, an age restriction. But what did 'total absorption' imply? Very long hours?

'It's a gas! Interesting job for someone with good speeds and telephone manner who wants to progress. Age late 30s-40s.'
Again, an ad for an older woman. But what sort of progress did this employer have in mind for someone in her forties?

'Super job for attractive young girl with typing and switchboard skills to work with masses of young men in City Business School.'
Accurate typing while answering calls is demanding; but you were supposed to trade this off against the access to young men. I wonder how many of them paid attention to the lucky applicant.

What were you supposed to make of 'Desperate young men are in urgent need of talented young secretaries,' 'She will gladden her boss's heart by her presence, her shape, her smile,' and 'An impeccably mannered cutie of a gentlewoman in her 30s'? (I'm still trying to work out what that one means.) And what on earth was, exactly, 'all-round experience'?

If the papers didn't turn up anything suitable, another option was to contact an employment agency. There were branches in every high street: Reed Employment, Alfred Marks Bureau, Kellys and Brook Street Bureau being the best-known. Agencies were often criticised for over-hyping placements, making them sound much more interesting than they actually were; but, apart from the obvious need to market vacancies effectively, part of the problem was that the employers couldn't explain what the secretary actually did because they didn't know themselves. So the ad was put together by someone in the company who had a vague idea and a bit of imagination and subsequently was creatively tweaked by the agency. The result was a work of fiction, the new recruit quickly became disillusioned and moved on — incidentally creating more business for the agency.

*****

How well paid was secretarial work? It's difficult to be precise about how much the 'average' secretary earned in the 70s because job titles were applied fairly loosely and many salaries were subject to negotiation. Benefits such as staff perks, bonuses, free products, subsidised meals and travel might also be available, and those working in public services in London were paid an additional supplement called London Weighting, which compensated for the higher cost of living in the capital. In my own experience, as a junior secretary in 1970 I earned around £950 per annum gross, roughly equivalent to that paid to nurses and non-graduate teachers. By 1979, in a job with more responsibility, my salary was £3,000. This sounds like progress, but steep rises in inflation during the decade eroded much of the value of this increase.

Of course a PA would have been better paid than me. By the late 70s, her salary would have been in the region of £5,000, to which benefits such as a company car and private health care might be added. She was paid at roughly the same rate as a new graduate manager, and about a fifth of what her boss earned before his benefits were taken into account.

Few companies allowed secretaries to join a contributory pension scheme — I was only offered this benefit by two employers: the quasi-Civil Service BBC and a German firm. However, the amount of paid annual leave rose during the 70s from two to three weeks, mostly to help companies retain staff at a time when pay rises had been disallowed. Two Public Holidays were added in England and Wales in the 70s, May Day in 1978 and New Year's Day in 1974. Until then, the first day of the year had been uniquely marked by staff struggling in, despite massive hangovers, to make a perverse point of principle.

*****

Before moving on to the processes involved in changing jobs, there is an important issue to consider. When I asked former secretaries whether they remembered any instances of discrimination at work, most replied that they couldn't and that they had always treated everyone equally. As one put it, 'Those issues were not something that we knew about, so it was never a problem. Except ability, if someone couldn't do the job then they'd be asked to leave.'

Although it was unlikely to be apparent to those already in the job, discrimination *was* practised in secretarial work. It took place at the point of recruitment. As we've seen from those ads, it was acceptable to specify the gender, age and even appearance of the desired candidate but, following the introduction of the Race Relations Act of 1968, illegal to refuse employment to a person on the grounds of colour or ethnic origin. Yet the vast majority of secretaries were white. How did this happen?

I can give an example. In the mid-70s, at a small company where I was working, a junior typist handed in her notice. My boss, who handled recruitment among other duties, told me to phone a couple of employment agencies and ask them to advertise for a replacement. From the replies, I was to meet five applicants, select two whom I thought were best suited to the job and ask them to return for a second interview with him. I was also instructed to tell the agencies not to send any 'black people', 'not because we are colour prejudiced, but we are a small firm and they wouldn't fit in here'. Technically, this wasn't illegal. It was not 'refusing' employment, it was just not offering it in the first place. Unaware of the legal requirements, I did what I was told, and when I passed this precondition on to the agencies no one seemed surprised. Of the five candidates I met, one was a well-qualified British Indian girl whom I shortlisted for the second interview, but she was not invited back. The other, a competent British white girl, was given the job.

And there were instances of discrimination in the workplace.

Anne Ballard
London

'The main division was what jobs were suitable for men and which for women. In particular in areas, like PR and advertising, there was age discrimination in the hiring of secretaries, but a relaxed attitude to gay and lesbian staff. Many offices were all-white and, if a black person was employed, there would be offensive comments about "smell" and so on.'

Wendy Gough
Midlands

'Initially there was no-one black or disabled in my office. I don't think they would have fared well in that climate. One girl had a West Indian boyfriend and the other girls ostracised her. Later on we did have a young Head of

Accounts who was Asian, and he had quite a lot of trouble establishing himself and getting any cooperation from certain staff. He won through because he was a brilliant character and in the end everyone loved him.'

Sarah Oram
London

'There wasn't a huge variety in ethnicities, although we had Asian people working in the accounts department. We did have one guy, and now I can't remember what his nationality was but he lost a parent at some point and he turned up at work one day with his head completely shaved except for a little topknot. Now, someone else who was also Asian took the piss out of him. He didn't realise I knew what it meant, and when I started getting angry he said, "Oh, you know what this means then?" And I said, "Oh, yeah". And I was annoyed with him because he really should have known better.'

Even in all-white offices it wasn't unusual for remarks to be made that were, at the very least, tactless.

Valerie Docker
London

'I had a bit of discrimination myself. Most people were positive about New Zealand, we supported Britain through the wars and so on, so I don't think they were anti-New Zealand; but people would talk about my New Zealand accent and say things like, "Oh well, it's not as bad as the Australians"'.

'In my first job one of the accountants said to me, "You know, when you phoned me up on the internal phone I couldn't understand a word you said!" They didn't like the fact that I didn't speak like them, and didn't mind saying so. They didn't think, "Oh, Valerie might be embarrassed" — because of course when you're only 19 you're embarrassed about almost everything, aren't you, you don't want to be singled out as different — in those days people were much more blatant about differences and commenting on them, and criticising someone from a different background.'

*****

Applying for a vacancy meant filling in a form on paper, or preparing a CV and letter in your best typing, which you then posted, and in those days you could expect an acknowledgement of receipt. Recruitment in larger firms was dealt with by a personnel department while at smaller ones it would be handled ad hoc, possibly by a one of the more experienced female members of staff.

If the company liked your application, the next step was to be invited for an interview. Early on in the 70s, it wasn't unusual to be asked to take a shorthand and typing test first, although thankfully this was never asked of me. Interviews consisted of anything from a perfunctory chat ending with, 'How soon can you start?' or 'Thank you, we'll let you know'; to being interrogated by a group of inquisitors lined up behind a huge mahogany desk in a room you never saw again.

Mary Ankrett
Walsall

'I remember being interviewed for the position in the printing company, it seemed my qualifications were not taken as proof of my ability and I had to take down dictation and type it back before the interview.

'I had only been married a year, and during the interview I realised that this man was suspicious of married women in the working environment. One of his statements was, "Married women only come to work to have affairs with their bosses", so I replied, "If you offer me the job, how long would it be before our affair would start?"

'At the time, I was working for the directors of a casino in Birmingham. It was a high class and very reputable organisation, run on the lines of Monte Carlo. His next statement was, "This company prints postage stamps and we have to be sure that anyone who works for us is very confidential and does not get involved in anything underhand. All night clubs deal in drugs and underhand business." In our case this was not true, and by this time I was thinking, "Do I really want to work for this man anyway?" I started to answer back because I felt insulted. My response was, "I did not realise you wanted me to work for 007. I am not an underhand person, and the people I am working for expect me to be professional and confidential in my work. Perhaps I might be better off looking for another job." The interview continued with him telling me more about the company and so on.

'When I left I thought that was the end of it, but the next day he telephoned me and asked, "When can you start?" I was surprised but decided I would give it a go. Although it had not been the kind of interview I had expected, it did give me an idea of the person I was to work for. He had not tried to appear any different than what he was, and we both knew where we stood. I continued to work for him for 11 years.'

Deirdre Hyde
London

'I had an interview once for a Personal Assistant vacancy in a film company in Berkeley Square. It was the first time I was asked to talk about things I was good at. So I told a few lies about myself and my experience, and then found myself saying I had developed a stunning serve in tennis, not quite matched by my backhand, but almost. Actually I hadn't picked up a tennis racket since leaving school at 16. Didn't get offered that job. Probably just as well.'

Michelle Metz
London

'Among the various interviews I experienced, two of them were particularly memorable for very different reasons. I was sent by my secretarial college to be interviewed for a job as a junior secretary in the office of the Duke of Edinburgh. I remember very little about the interview itself but asking the taxi to take me to Buckingham Palace did give me a thrill. I didn't get the job.

'By contrast, I went for another interview in a seedy office somewhere in Oxford Street. From what I recall there were two men present who seemed to be interested in a sheet of paper on which, strangely, there appeared to be printed black and white drawings of various sexual positions (or was I imagining it?). Alarm bells began to ring in my head. At the end of the interview I went down in the lift with another girl who was looking rather upset. I found myself wondering if something untoward had happened to her and what I had escaped from.'

Among the strangest questions asked at interviews were:

> -'Would your boyfriend mind if you had to work at weekends?'
>
> - 'Were you a prefect at school?'
>
> -'What is your favourite drink?' (to which the interviewee replied, "Gin and tonic" and got the job.)
>
> - "What's your star sign?"
>
> - 'What do you think of 1,000 year-old trees?
>
> - 'Do you believe in immortality?'
>
> - 'I'm thinking of offering you the job, but I'm not sure I could put up with you. I think you'd drive me mad. What do you think?'

If you arrived at a company just as it was starting up you might never have to undergo such questioning.

Tanya Bruce-Lockhart
London

'It's an awful thing to say actually, but I don't think I have ever had an interview.

'In 1968 it was announced in all the newspapers that LWT had got the contract for weekend TV programming. The company had been formed by a man called Aidan Crawley: John Freeman, Michael Peacock, Jimmy Hill, Humphrey Burton, Frank Muir, all the cream of the television world had bought into this brand new company. I thought, "Gosh this sounds interesting", so I turned up on a Monday morning at the General Electric Company just off Park Lane, where Arnold Weinstock had let LWT have two big offices for the about-to-join heads of Units, potential stakeholders and so forth.

'So, there I was. I went in and they said, 'Obviously we can't pay you much, but would you like to stay?" so I got taken on for a ridiculous amount of money, it was like a thousand a year and I thought, "My God! A thousand a year is a lot of money!" I thought the world was my oyster.

'You were employed there on the basis of whether you were any good or useful, but within half a decade that changed. Later on you had to have a degree and references and all kinds of things, it was much more competitive by then.'

Another bias in making appointments was that peculiarly British concern: social class. Remember Deirdre Hyde, at her first job interview, being asked what her father did? Family and educational background pretty much determined the level at which a secretary entered the hierarchy; working-class girls were shunted into typing pools and lower-level jobs, while middle- and upper-class ones took the rest. PAs, because they were likely to be in contact with people of status and wealth, were expected to be familiar with the correct social and business etiquette, and including in an advertisement the requirement for 'a pleasant speaking voice', ensured that only a higher-class girls with flawless Received Pronunciation would apply.

Val Docker
London

'I think that's the British disease, you always want to put people into a category. Not every country in the world does that. I see it because in New Zealand you're either a Good Bloke or you're not. Nobody really minds who your father was and if he went to Eton, it doesn't really matter. I've often looked at the way the British keep categorising people and I think it's such a shame and a waste of time, and it makes the British tense in certain situations. I've heard people ask questions at interviews as if they really meant, "Oh, what class were you born into?" and thought, "What does this matter? I thought we'd got past all this"'.

Ann Baker
London

'At an interview at the Tate Gallery I was asked which newspapers I read. I read what my parents read, but apparently the *Daily Mirror* didn't count. Didn't get the job. The Tate wanted young ladies, not girls from state schools living on council estates. Later I worked at the National Gallery for many years, running a secretarial team.'

Age mattered too. As we've already seen from the job ads, some bosses wanted to hire younger women, while others preferred those with more experience. Employers were also entitled to ask candidates how likely was it that they might become pregnant; after all, it wasn't until 1974 that family planning clinics were allowed to prescribe the contraceptive pill to single women.

Christine Allsop
Chesterfield

'I was told at one job interview by the boss that he would not be setting any more young women on as they always got pregnant, and therefore he would give the job to someone who was too old for children (i.e. in their 40s). I pointed out I was not even married and he just shrugged. I thought it was shocking at the time, but it was the norm.'

Secretaries with children found it particularly difficult to get a job. In the 1970s maternity leave, if it existed at all, was haphazard, extending to just a few weeks after the birth of a child. Nor was there much in the way of childcare, and a common request made of employers was to provide a crèche for the children of working mums. Doreen Ashpole became a secretary after training on a TOPs course.

Doreen Ashpole
Cambridge

'It was very enjoyable except for the commute and having to pay for child care, car parking, petrol so it took time to benefit from the income. For the first few years I was paying out more than I was earning. Luckily, I had a very good neighbour who had two boys the same ages as my two, she was pleased to earn some money. I could not have managed without her backup. Of course I tried to have my leave during school holidays, but it was not always possible. It was always difficult to manage time off to avoid deadlines and many times I worked through illness. In my first job, as an office junior, the two older ladies there didn't really like young Mums because they might bring in germs from the children.'

*****

Being employed as a temporary secretary, or 'temp', was a popular option for working mums. Employment agencies provided temps to companies to fill short-term vacancies that arose during staff holidays, a sudden spike in the volume of work or between appointments; also perhaps to Paul McCartney, who released an incredibly dreary song called *Temporary Secretary* in

1980. Assignments were usually weekly, less often for a few days or a couple of months. However, they weren't guaranteed employment, especially during the winter months, nor did they always receive holiday or sick pay. Nor were they well-paid. The company paid the agency by the hour for the temp's services, the agency deducted commission of at least 20 per cent and paid PAYE and insurance. The temp received whatever was left over, usually less than she would have done had she been a permanent member of staff in the same post. Temping was a handy solution for those who needed to fit their work around family commitments or who wanted time off every now and then to travel. It was also a useful way of finding a new job.

Germaine Greer, in her somewhat wonky paragraphs about secretaries in *The Female Eunuch,* claimed temps were liberating themselves by taking control, hiring themselves out when and where they pleased. Unfortunately she missed the point that it was not the temps who were in charge, it was the agency. They decided where, when and how often a temp was employed. However, there were benefits on both sides. Like the BBC attachment scheme, it was a handy way for secretary and company to try each other out. If they got on well together, and the post was vacant, she might be offered it permanently. In fact, it was often a much better way to get a job. The secretary was under no illusions about what the work would be like, and the company picked up a suitable employee without having to go to the expense of advertising and interviewing. Needless to say, the agency took a hefty commission on the arrangement.

Companies liked temps because as well as plugging odd gaps they often brought with them fresh perspectives and better working practices. As one of Silverstone's bosses put it, 'I sometimes get a better temp than my secretary, which can be very annoying'. On the other hand there was a risk of being landed with a duffer. One employer, whose temp had taken five days to finish a day's work, put in a claim against the agency and eventually, six months' later, received a credit for her services, but the majority didn't bother.

Janet Kingsland
London

'I temped all through the 70s. At one stage I worked in an agency: Paterson's in Poultry. I lived in Shoreditch, so 22 or 149 bus to the door. Every applicant was registered and, this was pre-computer, we kept a record of each temp on index cards. We used a code, so, for example, 'VNT' meant "Very neat and tidy", a red cross meant "Use only in an emergency". Sometimes 'reliable' would go on the card. All the girls were pretty good, so no complaints. We had one male shorthand typist, past retirement age but he came in on the odd occasion.'

I did several spells as a temp. No longer a salaried employee, I quickly became aware of the equation work = time = money: one hour of temping in the City covered the costs of my Tube fare plus half that of my lunch. Greer was right in the sense that it did give a whiff of independence. I turned up, did a good day's work and was paid for it; all without anyone expecting me to care about the sales manager's missing folder, whether Doris down the corridor had rung in sick for yet another week or the late arrival of the tea trolley. I wasn't asked for selfless devotion. Bosses viewed me with a mild curiosity or disinterest. At the end of each week I tidied my desk, said goodbye to everyone and never saw them again.

True, the other side of the coin was that I was part of the furniture, often parked in the darkest corner, given the oldest typewriter and the least interesting work. After all, nobody was going to waste more than the minimum amount of time explaining it to me, in fact, most of the time I was treated as if I was completely thick. This was a great relief. Bosses were always so appreciative when I handed in accurate work, and if not they didn't complain. They had expected nothing better.

Temping gave me an inside view of different businesses, from a solicitor's in the City of London, where I shared an office with a the fastest typist I came across, she used two fingers and had been there since before the war; an ad agency in Richmond, where I was deposited in a back office and, through a closed door, overheard an argument that culminated in savage threats and furniture being hurled about, before creeping out to lunch through an empty but devastated room; and an engineering company where the sales reps, having discovered that one of their team was gay, ostracised him and forced him into handing in his notice. I turned down the offer of a second week there.

Contributors provided some fascinating accounts of working as a temp.

Jenny Mustoe
London

'In the summer of 1971, during college break, I did a day and a half at Post Office Telecommunications. I sat in an open-plan office with everyone listening to cricket on the radio. Nobody spoke to me, beyond showing me to the desk with a manual typewriter and a large stack of paper to be typed up.

'I couldn't find the loo and was too embarrassed to ask, so I belted out at lunchtime to use the public ones nearby. When I announced that I had typed up all the work I was bid farewell with the parting comment that they had thought it would take me all week. I was just glad to get out of there.'

Valerie Docker
London

'I often thought about the waste, I mean, the waste of space and time and money. A lot of the jobs were there because the guy was in a position classified as needing a secretary. Most of the time I was under-employed and extremely bored, so that's when I read books or wrote my essays for the Open University.

'For a few weeks I worked for the Rothschilds and was party to conversations with a couple of members of the family which would be embarrassing to them now. I think because you were a secretary you weren't regarded as having ears. You couldn't be expected to understand.'

Heather Harvey
Hampshire

'I worked as a temp for the British Aircraft Corporation at Hurn Airport compiling the maintenance manual of the new One-Eleven. I didn't fully understand what I was doing, and have worried ever since about their safety.'

Jan Jones
Manchester

'The thing I always hated about temping was being the new girl every few weeks and always having to ask where everything was. There was one place out in the middle of nowhere where everyone was so unfriendly I used to sit in the loo to eat my sandwiches.

'I went to one job at an engineering company where they had obviously saved up all their awful work for the temp, so I spent a couple of days judiciously applying "sickly" make-up and never went back.'

Alison Chubb
London

'I did temp work for 18 months. I figured that if I didn't like a job I could just get the agency to give me another one the next day. I used to ask for work as an audio typist rather than a secretary as I hated shorthand. The pay was less but it was worth it as I would just be typing and wouldn't have any of that "outside a reasonable job description" secretarial stuff.

'The worst place I worked at was a cigarette manufacturer. They gave their employees free cigarettes and everyone in the typing pool chain-smoked all day. The job was just typing addresses on labels and the supervisor kept asking how many I'd done in case they weren't getting their pound of flesh.

'A boss at a house-building company had bad body odour and I hated having to go into his office as it stank. I opened the window in there one morning to air it and when he got in he was annoyed as the draught had made a couple of his papers fly round the room. Not long after he told me my services were no longer required. I knew exactly why this was — BO or no BO, I had seen him in the street with a young girl the night before and I sometimes picked up the phone when his wife rang.'

Carol Brinson
Sussex

'I enrolled as a temp which included a short time in a typing pool. The agency man apologised but said it would be "good for the soul". It was for an insurance company with an enormous office with rows and rows of desks. The big advantage was that it was on the sea front and in the summer, so lunch times saw me swimming and returning covered in sand and salt, while the other girls had all been busy painting their nails and doing their hair.'

If the boss risked being sent a duff temp, there was always a chance that she might be assigned the boss from hell.

Claudia Vickers
Newcastle

'I liked the variety. You could be in the typing pool one week and the Managing Director's office the next. There was more scope for sticking your neck out to suggest ideas and make changes as you knew you would not be there long. Somehow you were more often listened to.

'One boss I worked for had never had a full-time secretary, he couldn't keep them. I had agreed to stay there for seven weeks but tried to leave after one. He was a rude, unappreciative, grumpy man. When I booked the wrong lunchtime for a group of his visitors, not having been told there were two sittings, he deliberately berated me in front of them all. That was the sort of person he was. The agency was not in the least sympathetic — I got the impression every temp left that job asap — but if you let the agency down it felt as if you would not get another one. Agencies would send you to inappropriate places just to put someone there.'

A fourth, and much less common, way to find a new job was to be head-hunted.

Gillian Summers
London

'As we were drinking our coffee we (the secretaries) noticed an elderly gentleman in his office across the road drinking his. One day he raised his cup in salute, and we responded with the same. After a few weeks of this we saw that he had put up a notice with his phone number. After lots of giggles and nudges, I was the one nominated to make the call. He suggested we all meet him for lunch one day at the Golden Egg on Oxford Street.

'There began a lovely friendship. He was moving to work for Total Oil in the 3M building in Wigmore Street and he wanted me to be his secretary. This was much more fun, and the work ranged from drawing up huge tables on the typewriter (no mean feat) to arranging his aunt's funeral, and booking him and his wife a cruise on the ocean liner, the Mauritania.

Lorraine Oliver
Outer London

'The company I was at was taken over very suddenly and we were given no notice. This meant that the people still required would have to move to offices in the centre of London. I was unhappy about this, although I'd been offered a job. I was then approached by someone who had left the company some months before and was now General Manager of a TV lighting company, and he offered me a job as his secretary – just round the corner, more money, more status, only one person to work for.'

*****

Secretarial posts sometimes had attractive perks attached. The BBC offered a free copy of the *Radio Times* and membership of its sports and social club, well-remembered as a way of relaxing after work, meeting new people and finding out about the corporation.

Amanda Lunt
BBC London

'The weekly routine was much enhanced by membership of the BBC Club, an independently financed entity, run largely on the profits of its bars and buffets in BBC premises around the country. It boasted a vast array of sections devoted to all kinds of sports and other interests, from archery to wine-making, providing a chance to socialise and acquire skills in safe surroundings, and to find out what went on in other departments and what career opportunities might be on offer — what is nowadays known as networking.'

Then there were the celebrities one might bump into at any time.

Elaine Day
BBC, London

'I had a huge crush on Melvin Bragg, who presented a pilot show with us called *The Balloon Game*. Celebrity contestants had to argue in character as a person from history not to be metaphorically thrown out of a virtual balloon. Sadly it never went to series. To my embarrassment now I remember that if Melvin was in the bar I rushed to the loo to touch up my make-up and make sure I looked my best.'

Catherine Preston
BBC, London

'I shared a lift journey with Morecambe & Wise, they were just so naturally funny and had everyone in the lift in stitches. Far funnier than Little & Large when I saw them in the lift, all they could manage were scripted gags. By the way, I didn't just meet people in lifts, but those two journeys spring to mind.'

Now, how about travelling on a company executive jet?

Susan Coles
London

'I worked for a company based in Bond Street that managed pop stars like Tom Jones, Engelbert Humperdink and Gilbert O'Sullivan, but I never met them. It had an executive jet, a Hawker Sidley 125. Inside it was fitted out like a lounge, with comfortable seats facing each other in blocks of four, so that passengers could talk to each other in a relaxed way. I am not sure, but it sat maybe sixteen passengers. I was expected to work there when required. There was a cocktail bar on board from which I served drinks in crystal glasses. I don't remember having to go through the sort of channels we are used to now to get into other countries, perhaps there was a fast track for executive jet passengers. I did go to Libya, Amsterdam and Milan in this capacity.

'It was a boring job though, as I had to type the same letter over and over again (these were the days before word processors) and had to keep the boss supplied with Bourbon biscuits and made the tea and coffee. I did not stay long in this job.'

Corinne Korn
London

'When I worked at the travel agent I was able to get airline discount; when working at the large hotel I was able to stay at a hotel within the group in Paris.'

But not every job was this glamorous.

Christine Allsop
Chesterfield

'My only perks were the free stationery, i.e. envelopes, paper, pens, rubbers, etc., which everyone took home.'

*****

Being a secretary meant that it was possible to find work in other countries. Here are accounts from women who went to Germany, America and the Middle East, and another who attended a conference behind what was then the Iron Curtain.

Deirdre Hyde
Switzerland

'The *Daily Telegraph* supplied an advertisement from a Swiss import/export company in Zurich for English secretaries. I had done an evening class in German so felt qualified, with that and my French A-level. I had never been abroad, not even for a holiday. Or in fact lived away from home.

'There was no interview, I was just told to report to the offices in Zurich on such-and-such a date. I think they paid my travel costs. Certainly strange. I can't remember how my parents reacted, I'm sure they were worried, but they did organise accommodation for me through a friend of a friend.

'I caught the night train to Zurich. The offices were sparkling and new, and there were six or seven other secretaries, all different European nationalities, including an Irish girl. We all worked in one enormous brightly-lit room, with state-of-the-art electric typewriters and a bank of telex machines clattering away non-stop. Nothing could have been further removed from the dingy second-floor offices in Fleet Street with their clanking lift, wooden desks and manual typewriters. I can't remember if we had tea or coffee machines, but we all chain-smoked.

'There were three directors, all men of course, middle-aged Swiss Germans. And I had no idea what we were importing and exporting except it was mostly chemicals. My immediate boss was Herr K, who was not blessed with any social graces or charm and would just hand me my tape (we used transcription machines) every morning with a curt "Guten Morgen Fraulein". He patrolled our office constantly, and there was hell to pay if we were caught talking, or if we were a long time in the toilet he would knock on the door and ask us to hurry up.

'The day started at 8.00 am when we had to be at our desks, typewriters switched on and ready to go. Interesting that in Switzerland, desks/workstations faced towards the walls, rather than into the room, to discourage/stop chatter. We had a mid-morning coffee break when one of us would fetch coffees from a local cafe to drink at our desks. The lunch break was strictly half an hour. The entire secretarial staff switched off their machines and rushed to the nearest cafe. We had to be served promptly or else leave hungry because we didn't dare overstay our allotted time. We had no fixed typewriters-switched-off-and-coats-on finishing time; it was when the day's work was done and before the main post office, to where we had to take the mail, closed.

'Then we would often repair to the Silberkugel on the Bahnhofstrasse for a hamburger — unknown in UK at the time — or a bratwurst and a beer (interesting that I remember the food details) where we moaned bitterly about our employers and the various reasons why we were in Switzerland and why didn't we chuck it in.

'But chuck it in I did after about nine months, and returned to England just before my 21st birthday. I found the work culture here very different from Switzerland. No wonder they are such a prosperous nation.'

Hazel Rees
USA

'I applied for a secretarial position in Chicago with a company that obtained your green card, paid your air fare to America and found you a flat for one month. I flew out in February 1970 and worked there until November.

'It was very different in some ways to working in England. I was found a position in a small company owned by an elderly gentleman and run by his spinster Treasurer. The company was a small one and virtually everyone was first generation American or foreign. Ironically, my two bosses were both English but I was expected to call them "Mr" which seemed strange. I thought the USA was so much more relaxed about this. An American company had moved to my town in the 1960s and had caused great interest in that everyone was called by their first names. Not when I worked in Chicago!

'The owner once lectured me on the correct way to staple pieces of paper together. We didn't get paid if we were off work, although we did get free medical treatment. I was told that the men's toilets didn't have doors to make sure no one lingered. I shared a flat with two other English girls, several others lived in the same block, I think most of them worked in much more relaxed atmospheres.

'Because the company was involved with microwave technology we had a microwave oven in the kitchen/rest room, this was the first time I had seen such a thing. In fact I didn't have one until about 1982 after my marriage and even then it was a new technology in England.'

Gillian Summers
Bahrain

'Soon after my arrival [in the Middle East] my father sorted out a job for me with a friend of his who owned a chain of department stores. I did not realize initially that he actually didn't need a secretary at all, his Indian minions were more than capable of typing his letters and keeping his diary. However, in those days it was a great status symbol for an Indian shop-owner to have an English secretary.

'In the first few months I had very little to do, and wandered round the store getting in the way of the senior managers, so my boss decided that I should amuse myself by creating a luxurious office for him to entertain his business visitors. I enjoyed spending someone else's money, and created a lovely room with a deep red carpet, a huge desk with a comfortable leather chair and a small coffee table in one corner with two soft easy chairs for his little tête-à-tête with his visitors. He loved it.

'But I still had nothing to do, so his next ruse was to get me to visit all the other top business owners to persuade them to advertise in his social magazine. Every morning I would visit their offices, where the norm was to arrive and join the queue in the reception room (Majlis) and move along one seat at a time until it was my turn to speak to the top man. I was always the only woman (girl) and, with my short skirts and bare legs, was quite a sight for the other visitors who were all dressed in traditional Indian or Arab robes. I always got my advertisements as it would have been churlish for them to refuse in front of all the other waiting visitors.

'He was terribly proud of being a Mason and there were no secrets about it, so another job I was given, when he became Master of the Lodge, was to organize his Ladies' Night and choose a gift for each lady from his store. Powder compacts, pearl necklaces and pure silk handkerchiefs were favoured.

'I was never asked to take dictation or to type anything more than a bill of exchange, but one thing that I found fun was entertaining all the visiting salesmen from the UK, Ireland, France and even America. I would meet them when they arrived, show them around the store, sit them in the plush office and send out a boy (peon) to bring Pepsi or whatever they requested and chat to them while we waited for Mr. J to turn up, which was sometimes a long time as in the Middle East punctuality is not seen as a virtue. I got to know some of them well and they would often give me samples of their wares – I still have a lovely silk scarf from a French perfume company.'

Terry Kaye
Poland

'During the conference season we [at Beechams] needed to go to Poland. So we drove there through Hungary and Czechoslovakia. When we got to the Polish border they kept us waiting forever while they checked the paperwork. Eventually I said to my boss, "Is it because I've not been here before?" And he said, "Yep, possibly." Eventually we got the go-ahead. It was a curious experience, I must say. It felt a bit eerie.

'At the hotel, all of one floor was dedicated to foreigners. I learned a few tricks though. I knew there was a microphone in the bathroom so I used to make extra loud noises in the toilet for them. Very juvenile I know, but it made me feel better.'

*****

So far we have looked at what was involved in finding new employment, but what about the other end of job-life, what happened when you left a job?

In the normal run of things you typed out a nice letter of resignation and told everyone the news, hoping they showed at least a tinge of regret at the news of your impending departure. If your employer was willing to pay two salaries for a few days (most weren't) you had time to hand over to your successor and give her the low-down on things like the equipment that needed a good kick before it functioned, how many sugars the boss took in his tea and which people were best avoided after lunch. As we know, it was highly unlikely that anyone else in the company had much idea about what you had been doing there, least of all your boss so, in the absence of a handover, you typed out your "will", a document with the same information, possibly including an instruction to destroy after reading. If, when you arrived at your new job, there was no will waiting for your attention, you were usually confronted by your new boss sighing hopefully, 'Well, I'm not sure what Sue actually did, but the reports used to come out every Monday'. From then on you used your imagination, searched through the files or consulted the mafia for Sue's new phone number.

Departure day signalled certain rituals: lunch with the boss followed by afternoon tea or an evening in the bar with your workmates at which you would be presented with a card signed by them all saying how much they would 'Miss you!!! xxx'. If you had been a long-term inmate you might receive a leaving present, from which you could immediately infer the level of your colleagues' esteem: a pack of notelets was not a good sign. However, if the circumstances of your departure were controversial you would be unlikely to get anything at all. The only option then was to wreak your revenge by looting the stationery cupboard.

There was another scenario to leaving a job: dismissal. In 1977, after I had been working for a year in Mayfair for a Regional Sales Manager, I was called into his office and told that the company had decided to 'restructure'. This was a term I hadn't come across before. Apparently we had to quit our plushly-carpeted and mahogany-fitted building and my boss was to be 'relocated' — another new word — to an office in Limehouse, East London, a prospect which, as a former Guards' officer, filled him with terror and despair. In a half-hearted way he mentioned the possibility of my transferring with him but, as I was living at the opposite end of the District Line, it wasn't very tempting. I was told I would receive a month's pay and could leave without having to work my notice.

It was a January afternoon. Back in my office, I stared out of the window at a grey and drizzly Berkeley Square, watching lights being switched on, letting the news sink in. I'd spent seven years trying to find a job that suited me and, just as I had, it was being taken away. I realised that the suggestion of moving to East London was a formality so the company could say they had offered me something and I'd refused it. I packed up my desk and trudged to Green Park station.

No experience is ever wasted. Losing that job taught me a very important lesson about how soul-destroying it is for anyone to be made redundant. However long and enthusiastically you work for an employer, if he wants to get rid of you, he will. So, assuming you have a contract at all, read it with care. The loyalty your employer owes you is in the termination clause.

Gill Bazovsky
Swansea

'Redundancy happened very suddenly and unfairly; the directors had brought some people down from London to talk to the staff about pensions only the week before! I was lucky, because although I hadn't been there long enough to receive redundancy pay I got some holiday pay. Other staff members were poorly served and had to go on the dole.'

Olwen Hanson
Yorkshire

'There were major organisational changes resulting from company mergers and the head office function moving. As the other site already had senior management with the necessary support, including secretarial, my role no longer existed. There were suggestions that I may like to take on a role at the other site, but this was not an option for me. Somewhat ironically, the company did move the senior management function back to the site I had worked at within 18 months – and "my job" was advertised!'

Claudia Vickers
Newcastle

'I was dismissed by being asked by my boss if I had ever wanted to travel. "Well," he said, "have the afternoon off and go and book your ticket today!"

'Looking back, any relationship had completely broken down as he was flirting (and probably not all?) with another girl in the same room. He had a lovely wife with small children.'

Thinking about leaving jobs reminds me of those strange occasions when you went back to visit a place where you had once worked. You might have spent years there, but once you had gone the waters closed behind you. Within a week your name was no longer mentioned; a year on and you were forgotten. What had been 'your' desk, chair and typewriter now belonged to someone else; and the dried up pot plants you had left behind were now thick with big, green, glossy leaves.

Valerie Docker
BBC London

'I noticed that a lot of his former secretaries kept coming back, and he wasn't always totally pleased to see them — just in the sense he was very busy. So I thought to myself, I won't do that. I won't come back and visit him.'

Wendy Gough
Midlands

'I remained friends with one girl from my first job at the insurance company, and I did go back to collect her from work for a night out, but it was a bit weird. I felt glad not to be working there, felt older than the girls I knew before, somehow. Same old faces doing the same old grind. People were not very interested in talking. I think that people lose interest in people outside their immediate sphere. You become out of context somehow.'

*****

Through the 70s, the job carousel whirled round and round and thousands of happy and helpful secretaries joined and left, every job the same but different. But as the years passed, the roundabout gradually began to slow down. Eventually it stopped altogether.

You remember that one reason for focussing on the 70s was because it was the last decade before automation changed the world of work forever? In the final chapter we'll see how that took place.

Chapter 8 : A history of the future

It's August 1977. I am working as a temp for IBM in their classy new offices near Putney Bridge in West London. I am typing, on a Golfball (yay!), a sales proposal for the lease of some computers to a company in the Great North Road. I have little understanding of the technology involved and have to stop and check the files of previous correspondence every now and again to make sure I am using the correct terms. It is 2 hours and 27 minutes to go before the lunch break.

The door opens. In trundles the postman, the IBM postman that is. From the box on his trolley he removes the morning's letters, hands them over and watches as I open the envelopes.

"You do know," he says in a low and confidential voice, "that soon you'll be out of a job."

"Of course," I reply. "I'm a temp."

"Nah, I don't mean that," he retorts. "Sekketris, you know, and all that ... typing you do. Offices are going paperless. All down to computers, you see. There'll be no need for you."

An emphatic nod. Out he trudges. Well mate, think I, if that's so, you too.

My lack of concern about this imminent obsolescence might have been because office technology seemed immutable. Had I been teleported back from the 70s to the 1920s I would have found recognisable typewriters, shorthand notebooks and filing cabinets, and would have had little difficulty settling in. However, had I been projected forwards 50 years to one of today's offices, I would have arrived in a different world altogether.

I had heard about the 'paperless office', it had been talked about for some time, along with other futuristic mumbo-jumbo about office automation, the information society and knowledge workers. But it was a mystery to me how we were supposed to get from wire basket in-trays and manilla folders to desks with flashing lights in rooms with airlock doors. (We assumed offices of the future would look this: *Star Wars* came out that year.) I knew about computers too, those enormous 'electronic brains' that did clever calculations, ran stock controls and payrolls and made terrible mistakes, like paying someone £2.50 instead of £250 or sending goods for London W1 to the West Indies. Had I done something like that I would have been fired. And these servers had to be housed in air-conditioned, dust-free chambers! Unlike us secretaries, working in thick smoke and temperatures varying from Siberian to Saharan. Anyway, computers couldn't even make a decent cup of tea: how would they replace us?

*****

It began with a false start. In 1966, Ulrich Steinhilper, World War Two Luftwaffe ace and IBM typewriter salesman, proposed to his senior managers that the company should develop a system to automate document production. At first, the concept seemed bizarre and was dismissed. It took him five more years of persuasion before he came up with a term they could grasp, 'word-processing' (WP). Now it made sense to the guys who had done well out of data-processing.

WP was originally conceived as a completely new way to produce office documents, and was marketed as such, even though initially it simply repurposed existing equipment. To begin with, the idea was to get rid of all the pesky secretaries and typists. Instead, using numerical code commands, the boss would dictate material down a landline phone to an automatic typewriter modified to act like a telegraph machine — technology that had been around since 1917 — and have it printed out. No shorthand, audio or copy typing would be required. Business journals were appraised, articles in trade journals appearing hailing WP as the exciting new future which would revolutionise the office forever. One of the bosses interviewed by Rosalie Silverstone had probably read one of them when he told her, 'At the moment [secretaries] are indispensable because we haven't any other means of communication. If a machine were invented instead of shorthand-typing they would become superfluous.[42]"

How were IBM to persuade prospective customers to take this on? After a some experiment, they modified their process. Bosses would now dictate to audio cassettes, with which many were already familiar, and companies would move a bunch of their secretaries into 'word-processing centres' where, as highly trained 'specialists' earning pay commensurate with their skills, supervised by 'experts', would play them back and type out the material on new and more efficient machines. The remaining secretaries could be let go. WP would make document production as efficient as the assembly line had the manufacture of goods. "Do this", they said, "and your productivity will be boosted by 500-1000 per cent!"

Managers, who for years had considered that office investment meant simply hiring another secretary and buying another typewriter, had little or no data with which to compare this proposal, but they could see that it would mean abandoning the traditional model of one-boss/one-secretary/one-typewriter. Was this really necessary? IBM helped them to decide by referring them to feminism. The old ways of working are outdated and demeaning, they said, and the women are trapped and bored. You can see an interesting example in a promotional film made by the company in 1975 where it is claimed that, 'the office is like an old-fashioned Victorian family with father and domestic servants doing go-fer duties', adding that a (unnamed) 'scholarly study' showed a typist on average only achieved four to six words per minute.[43] (Presumably because she was engaged in other duties much of the time.) One Walter Kleinschrod, editor of Word-Processing Reports, found secretaries might spend as little as 2 per cent of their time taking dictation and 19 per cent of it typing and proofing documents; evidence which, he suggested, proved their typing wasn't up to much. Moreover, to Walter's annoyance and frustration, it was very hard to control what these women were doing[44] It was true that much of what secretaries did could not be accurately assessed, who could put a price on being happy and helpful, or knowing how many sugars the Head of Accounts took in his tea? But also, perhaps, some executives were chilled at the thought of losing the women on whom they had relied to carry out much of their duties for them, and to keep them out of trouble too.

In practice, WP as a wholesale restructure tended not to take place. It was expensive, and existing procedures were often too complex and fragmented to allow it to be implemented in full, especially when office politics joined the discussion. Instead, it tended to be implemented gradually and piecemeal. Senior managers, adamant they weren't going to send off confidential documents to a typing pool, retained their secretaries and provided them with updated machines such as IBM's MT/ST and its successors. In the time saved, their newly titles 'executive assistants' were able to carry out more varied and interesting administrative duties.

Even had they been consulted about the proposed changes, I am not sure secretaries could have, or even would have, argued against them. There were big advantages in using WP machines, the most welcome being that, at, last, mistakes could be corrected before a document was printed — less swearing, more jokes about plastering the screen with Tippex. Serial documents, such as quarterly accounts, could be formatted and retrieved when needed, rather than typed from scratch every time. Standard letters could be merged with files of multiple addresses instead of each one being typed separately; draft documents could be shared and amended, rather than repeatedly typed, printed and circulated. Saving documents electronically (theoretically) removed the need for paper copies to be filed in cabinets, although in practice most places kept them, just in case. Younger bosses preferred to record dictation on cassettes and hand them to whoever was available for typing, rather than wait for a particular secretary to be free to take notes in shorthand.

As the decade progressed, further refinements by IBM and its competitors came onto the market. Keyboards acquired VDUs (visual display units) allowing on-screen menus and prompts, and were linked to storage stations and daisywheel printers. Floppy disks appeared. One secretary remembers being hugely excited when she moved from a "one-line WP to a WP that could *gasp* save a WHOLE document!" Bosses, some reluctantly, started to use networked machines to share projects and calendars. Eventually, instead of signifying a new system of work organisation, word-processing came to mean software programs for onscreen text editing.

Chris Green
Feltham, Middx

'The first time I saw a word processor was when I went back to work in the late 70s. I thought, "What on earth is this?" Eventually, after looking at it for a while, I was brave enough to switch it on. And once I got the hang of it I found out that when you made a mistake it was easy to fix. That was a real step forward.'

Patricia Robb
Ottawa

'IBM came out with the mag card memory typewriter, the MT/ST. There was a small screen where it would display one line at a time. It also saved the document on a magnetic card, which you could feed into the machine and go back line by line to make corrections later if your boss decided he wanted a change. Only one person in the office had one and she was the envy of all the secretaries.'

Sarah Oram
London

'Change happened at a different pace in different companies. One of the ways to copy documents for someone else was to save them to what was then one of those large floppy disks and give them that. In the 1980s, the firm I worked for had offices across the globe and used an early form of email to exchange messages called EMess, but there was no idea that it could be used more generally. As far as making appointments, doing the correspondence, doing the filing, making travel arrangements, organising this and that, it was much the same.'

There were disadvantages to WP. Those word-processing centres needed good typists who could spell but were never bored — a rare combination. Secretaries who were moved into them resented losing the more interesting parts of their work and felt they had been turned into machines themselves. After all, these centres were typing pools in all but name and had the same old problems: lack of communication with the author of the work, noisy, cramped surroundings, poor levels of pay (those specialist salaries never materialised) and limited social interaction. Even worse, as the middling-level jobs were eliminated, there was less possibility of promotion.

It wasn't just the word-processing operatives who were unhappy. As the speed with which the personal secretary could produce documents increased, she found herself presented with more work or made responsible to a couple more bosses, which placed her in the firing line when they all wanted their own work given priority. Once the link to a single boss had been broken, it became more difficult for her to keep on top of everything around her. Moreover, secretaries, who for decades had taken a pride in turning out top-quality work at short notice, were frustrated by having to slow down and learn the completely new ways of operating WP machines, while their bosses were baffled, as they had been told how much easier their work would become. As an example, even though the most common WP programs, WordPerfect and WordStar, included options for set and variable layouts ('fool/trick/reset') some secretaries felt the creativity they had enjoyed using in laying out complex documents, with tabulations, columns and sub-sub-paragraphs, had been taken away without any consideration for their former achievements. They had lost control. And standards were slipping.

Sarah Oram
London

'In the paper-based days you'd send out a draft document for comment with a deadline for replies, and you had to hit that deadline because you would need to re-type the final version, get it photocopied and circulated before, say, the meeting. Once computers came in, documents could go on being revised up to the last minute, which was useful; but the downside was there was less time to check the final version. Mistakes started to creep in.'

Hazel Rees
London

'My main bugbear at the end of my secretarial life, before I retired in 1990, was the decline in good English and letter layout. More and more standard letters were created in the system, and care was not always taken to ensure the relevant words/sentences were amended/deleted as appropriate. Despite spellchecker some real howlers were sent out! However I am on my hobbyhorse. I meet up about once a month with an ex-colleague and we are always exchanging faux pas we have seen.'

Typists, stuck in front of WP machines all day, complained about back and eye strain from peering at the screens. And there was another, more serious problem. How far repetitive strain injury (RSI) was a physical condition specific to the introduction of computer technology, and how far it was a manifestation of the problems of adapting to new work practices is unclear; but the condition was serious enough to terminate working lives.

Heather Pippins

'I retired when I was 56 because I was shot to pieces with repetitive strain injury. I'm still struggling, I can't hold cups and saucers.

'It was as a result of computers. When I was using manual and electric typewriters it was fine. When the desktop computer came in, we were not allowed to have a mouse because the computer whizz-kid had worked out that we were quicker using the keyboard. No wrist rest, no ergonomic chairs, and my console was stood up on telephone books. I was in a senior position and there were three of us. We were guinea-pigs, no two ways about it.

'I would go home at night crying with pain across here [indicates shoulders] and down my arm. I went to work for two years with one of those support things, but I took the steel pin out so I could still type. I was in a terrible state and I thought, I have got to stop. And one of the best bits about it was that I was also secretary to the Health and Safety Officer!

'I had terrible arguments with my boss. I said, "Look, I am as fast as you need me to be on an electric typewriter". And this ... idiot said, "If you sue the company you're no use to me. I'll get rid of you." And that was one of the reasons I thought, "This is it, I'm going to retire now, even though it affected my pension".'

By the end of the 80s, personal computers incorporating word-processing programs as part of their package, began to supplant WP. Word-processing centres closed and offices went back to producing their own documents, only this time it was the turn of the bosses, few of whom had learned touch typing, to do the work. Strangely, it was another secretarial duty that disappeared altogether; call centres got the job of 'manning' the phone.

Barbara Rich
London

'I remember early 1980s' offices where the boss had the latest model of desktop computer not on his desk but just for show, pristine under a cover on a little table. His secretary would be sitting outside his office, busy typing away on a not-the-latest-model.

'I do still come across the occasional older male solicitor who asks his secretary to type an email for him, and feel that's anachronistic. Even in recent years I've had emails sent to me by solicitors' secretaries, which have been dictated to them by a fee-earner who can't type.

Lucy Fisher
London

'Yes, even 20 years ago, the exec. had his computer on a side table (very uncomfortable) not on his BIG DESK. They couldn't understand that it was there so we wouldn't have to retype their stuff! Once I made someone very grand type on an early laptop while his blokes looked on in horror.'

Rosemary Kaye
Not disclosed

'When I went back to work in the early 2000s, the archaic law firm I joined had only just got computers, one for each of the two partners and one for the cashier. The rest of us had none. One of the partners sent hers back and said she didn't want to bother with it, perhaps a sixth sense warned her against the evils of procrastination on the internet.

'Even in the last law firm I worked for, which was much more up to date than the one I mentioned, the partners still had personal secretaries and hardly knew how to use their own laptops. This was in 2009!'

Even today a Managing Director, described by one of his staff as 'a dick who is stuck in the past,' dictates his emails to his PA.

But what became of personal secretaries? It turned out that, after all, they were useful. They became Executive Assistants, handling administrative duties. As one former member of staff at IBM wrote, ' A good portion of them were magically promoted to management in the late 70s, when the push to fast-track women and minorities was in full swing. You were working in branch offices for a branch manager, and then in a few short years — poof! You are now management material, memorize these lines!'

Judith Farnell
Yorkshire

'At the end of the 70s I moved to working for a partner in a large firm of chartered surveyors. I don't think the work actually changed but I did have a lot more responsibility and thrived in that professional atmosphere. I was allowed to, and encouraged to, take on much more responsibility. I became a true PA rather than a secretary.'

Along with technology, office culture changed too.

Wendy Gough
Midlands

'My first job, despite it being in 1976, was like working in the 1960s. In 1979 I went to the local planning authority. It was a more varied role. There was much less scrutiny of dress, and I wore denim, although there was still a typing pool and the chief officer's secretary was still ruling the roost.

'The 1980s were very different. In the late-1980s, I had an office job in a box manufacturing company and left after becoming pregnant. When my son started school I wrote asking for a reference and they invited me to go back to work there.

'I regretted it very much. The company was much less friendly. This was the time of the yuppie, and everything was very competitive and back-biting. I seemed to be the only employee with a child, and was given a part-time contract with no holiday or sick pay which is illegal now but I needed the flexibility. I suppose it was a bit like the zero hours arrangements of today. The bosses made it difficult sometimes for me to leave on time to do the school run. I left after 18 months.

'Young people cannot understand why our generation did not have careers: lack of childcare and not being a man accounts for most of it. I do wonder how women managed. Back then, there were very few nurseries and no childcare for school age children. Of course these women who were forced to take time out to look after their children are now having years added to their pension age.'

Hazel Rees
London

'I think things changed considerably in the late 80s and 90s, towards the end of my time as a secretary. The pressure of work built up. Technology had advanced so that everything was wanted straight away. People became impatient. Staff numbers were cut and those that remained were expected to be available at home as well at work. When people were away no one was available to take up the slack. More staff worked part-time (often because of legislation allowing returning mothers to work part-time instead of full-time) which had a knock-on effect on efficiency and caused stress to other staff members.'

Deirdre Hyde
London

'There was maybe a slightly more relaxed attitude between bosses and secretaries. Maybe. Also the dress code changed. All advantages; except the demise of the tea trolley, as we had to make our own drinks and, of course, clear up. And buy our own biscuits.'

Phyllida Scrivens
London

'Later on in my career I supervised my own secretary. The possibilities of travel increased, whether it simply be to supervise a training conference, or maybe accompanying bosses on overseas trips (not that I ever did!). Organising a diary or arranging travel became far easier.

'But as for the paperless office dream! That has never happened — we would print everything and file it away just as we had always done.'

So had it been a waste of time mastering typing and shorthand? Had Frances Cairncross been right all along?

The need to learn keyboard skills is disappearing with the use of voice commands and text messaging — how delighted Ulrich Steinhilper would have been to hear that, were he alive today. But even if touch typing is a dying skill, it has been of enormous value to those who have used it.

Alison Chubb
London

'Everyone types on computers now, but strangely no one seems to be taught to touch type or takes the initiative to learn it themselves. Do they not realise how much quicker and easier on the eyes it is? I used to be made to feel that I was wearing a large label saying "slowest typist in the world," but more recently, when I was copy typing some lengthy thing I caught my boss staring at me in awe at how much faster I could type than she could!'

Chris Green
Feltham, Middx

'Nowadays bosses do their own typing although, as they were never taught how to do it, they're all [mimes two-finger typing]. I can remember people coming into my office and you're having a conversation while typing, and they say, "How come you can talk and type at the same time?" But that's just what we did. All that time they're wasting doing this [two-finger typing].'

Although filing paper copies was one of the (understatement klaxon) least absorbing parts of secretarial work, the skill needed to create a system for sorting and storing documents in places where there was a strong chance of being able to find them again turned out to be very useful for personal computers. But poor old shorthand is fading fast. It isn't even a keyboard on the app store. The last reported sightings from contributors were from 1987, both from secretaries who failed shorthand tests for jobs: one at the National Gallery in London and the other working for the Labour politician, Robin Cook. Today it survives as a cult interest. One former secretary uses it to jot down notes from phone conversations, a former shorthand teacher posts intriguing examples on Twitter.

As I write, the whole future of offices is being questioned as so many more people have been working from home during the Covid-19 lockdown. The open-plan office is still with us, although the emphasis today is less functional, based on creating environments that reflect the natural world and promote wellness and creativity. Glass walls and atriums flood buildings with light; interior spaces are divided by a minimum of structures into separate areas for different purposes: desks with a screen, keyboard and backboard, clear desks, white tables for hot-desking, comfy couches with coffee tables, cubicles for silent working and meeting rooms. Instead of corridors with linoleum floors, walls are decorated with super-large blow-up photos and spaces brightly coloured, reminiscent of primary schools. Shower rooms mean, in theory, there is no need now to sit near a smelly colleague. Coffee bars and food stations with microwave ovens and kettles have replaced the old-style canteens, and there may even be a roof garden in which to take a break, if the sun is shining.

Some things haven't changed much though. Senior managers have their own offices, a few filing cabinets stand guard beside enormous pot plants and if, back in the 70s, clocking-in was regarded as a laughable relic, it's been revived in the form of the security check-in, the ID card hanging on a lanyard.

One of the most significant changes has been in the apportioning of personal workspace. Back in the 1970s it would be highly unlikely that you would have shared a desk with anyone else. Today, hot-desking prevents what is now called 'nesting', staff claiming personal space for themselves, presumably to save space and costs. For the employee, this means there is no guarantee of being able to sit in the same place each time at work, or even of finding a place at all and, if the members of a team are called for a meeting, there may not be sufficient room for them all to gather. Without a desk, personal items are stored in lockers, again like schoolchildren. One current government worker reported that sitting in rows at hot desks made her feel like a battery chicken. Does this remind you of the typing pool? Me too.

I wondered whether we could ascertain how far today's office workers differed from their 1970s' counterparts by asking them what they kept in their desks (at least, those who still had them). So I asked the Twitter hive-mind to list the contents of their drawers. Here is what today's 'average' office worker keeps in his/her desk:

> An apple (possibly), Blu Tack, business cards (for contacts who have probably have left their company), cables and chargers (for phones you don't have), calculator, carrier bags (folded), coffee pods or jars, a deerstalker hat, dental floss, deodorant (for emergency use), giant scarf (for when the office is cold), gym kit, handcream, headphones (for video calls), hi-vis jacket (for fire drills), highlighter pens, hole punch, a jar of pickles, letters from HR, mug, pants (spare), paracetamol, pen (that doesn't work), pot noodles, rubber (old), ruler, scissors (blunt), shoes, socks (spare), staff handbook, stapler, sweets (emergency), tampons, tie, tights, tissues, training handouts and treasury tags (still used in solicitors' offices).

Around half of those items would have been in my desk drawer in the 1970s, so maybe, even if their surroundings have changed, the personal world of the office worker hasn't changed quite as much. And how surprising it is that so many pieces of equipment whose only function could be associated with paper are still there. That IBM postman would be so disappointed. I also asked someone currently working in a school, and previously in a solicitor's office, what she thought about the paperless office.

> 'We have paper copies of student files — everything from health questionnaires to the emails sent back and forth as part of the admissions process — and they all get filed away for a set period (I think at least six years) after the student leaves before they can be sent to a confidential waste company to be destroyed securely. That makes it sound like hazardous material or something, but GDPR and data security is a big thing.

> 'At the solicitor's, I archived about a thousand files when our office merged with a smaller firm and HOO BOY some of those were old and dusty enough to make me

sneeze. But they were still being worked on so they had to be kept somewhere safe. I think there were files there older than me.'

Maybe the paperless office is another myth too?

*****

We are reaching the end of our journey through the 70s, but there's time for a quick look back with our former secretaries to find out what they think now about their former job.

The majority agreed that it had given them experience and knowledge that they would not otherwise have had. Those from traditional working-class backgrounds, whose families had worked in factories and shops, were particularly proud of what they had achieved and said it gave them opportunities and the confidence to socialise at any level of society. 'And money!' said one. 'What do you go to work for except to earn money?'

On the other hand, there were regrets. One contributor felt there had been very little that was tangible to show for her work. 'My husband was a painter and decorator and when he finished a job he could see something concrete for his labours, a well-decorated room or gleaming woodwork, but secretaries did not have this sort of job satisfaction.' Others wished they had asserted themselves more, or pushed themselves to do better.

Mary L Cryns
San Francisco

'I was happy because I made more money than pretty much all my friends at that time! By age 20 I was able to get my own apartment in San Francisco and live independently, which was fabulous. I was learning to do all kinds of stuff as a legal secretary because my attorney was teaching me and he wasn't as scary as I thought he would be.

'I mainly loved to type and do transcription. What really changed for me was becoming a word-processing Technician and learning all the advanced technical skills and going with the flow on all the changes. I loved that so much! And because I've been a secretary, I've always been able to jump in and help the secretaries with things as well.

'Although over the years I'd think, "Oh man, I want to be a teacher or a writer, or something". But this is what I do. It's who I am and I'm okay with it now.'

What became of these former secretaries? Many went on to other things after the 1970s, among them: a university tutor with a doctorate in English Literature, an award-winning biographer, a social worker and partner in a mediation company, the owner of a family business selling souvenir memo blocks, a surveyor for cavity wall insulation, a speech and language therapist working with pre-school children, a national level first aid trainer and a potter. This impressive list shows how myopic were those old assumptions about what girls were capable of achieving; but maybe too it shows how valuable the disciplines of working as a secretary had been, and how useful the experience.

Let's begin with **Tanya Bruce Lockhart,** whose 'goat' Rikki caused such controversy. She went from being Frank Muir's secretary to researching for programmes on London Weekend Television. Later she produced documentaries for *The South Bank Show,* the longest continuously running arts programme on UK television. Latterly she joined Granada Television to head up arts programming there and was instrumental in bringing the ballets of choreographer Kenneth Macmillan to ITV. She now runs the popular and highly respected Bridport Literary Festival, currently in its sixteenth year.

> 'Although at the time I thought, "Oh God, I'm going to be a secretary", but I have never regretted becoming one because, even if everybody regards you as the lowest of the low, you have to be organised because the person you work with may not be. In every job I've had since I've been organised, to the point that I'm hopeless at delegating. I'm endlessly list-making. Still, every morning I list the tasks, people to ring, people to write to; the discipline that I learned at Mrs Hoster's stood me in good stead. If you were energetic and proactive and you contributed, it was a wonderful springboard to other things.'

As you may remember, **Gwen Rhys** started out from South Wales with the ambition of running her own business and quickly became a PA.

> 'Being PA to the MD gave me a huge amount of confidence when speaking to senior people, and a great deal of autonomy and responsibility. At the top level it gave me an insight into running a business.
>
> 'From late 1970s to 1987 I ran a word-processing bureau. I then spent nearly ten years developing initiatives throughout the UK to raise expectations and educational attainment of young people. This led to my being Chief Executive of a business development agency, which led to my setting up a network of female entrepreneurs, which led to me developing a personal brand, which led to my setting up an award-winning organisation that champions gender diversity.'

Catherine Preston, who began by learning to type at Sight and Sound in Oxford Street, also ended up running her own company.

> 'I learned something every day, and used that new skill each time to further my career. I became the boss of my own company 20 years later when the existing company head died suddenly and the vultures pounced to grab what they could. I was running a division within it by that stage. When it all fell to pieces, and with the encouragement of my (personal) partner, I set up a new company. I contacted all my clients, changed the letterhead and that was it.'

> 'Being MD allowed me to appoint and nurture new recruits and young secretaries, treating them well and bringing out the best in them. Most of my ex-staff still get together as a family from my company to reminisce; not bad, as I sold up in 2002. Seems I got staff relations right! Good female boss! Teamwork, responsibility, life skills, typing was the start of everything I have achieved. It's amazing where a typing course can take you.'

Secretarial work brought **Anne Ballard** from Canada to London, and then on to qualifying as a solicitor.

> 'It got me away from a country where I was unhappy, and enabled me to earn a reasonable salary while I decided where my life was going; let me test what suited me and what didn't. I regret my early lack of education and not being encouraged to think seriously about a proper career, but I am very glad the secretarial option was available when I needed it. And I met some interesting people and made some good friends along the way. In my first two jobs I had my own secretaries: usually three or four to a room who helped each other when one got busy. I made

friends with them and one went on to qualify as a solicitor too.

'We live in a different world now, and for women in work it's a much better one.'

Elaine Day made the transition from television secretary to media producer.

'I applied for training in what was considered the next step up from secretary in production, in those days called a Production Assistant – again almost solely female because they would have had to be secretaries first. The job varied, depending on the genre of programme making, but in drama encompassed supporting the Director in every aspect of the production process from casting to post-production, including on location and in the studio gallery.

'In the mid-80s I was lucky enough to be offered a freelance role doing continuity on a feature film, and left the BBC. It was who you knew and word of mouth. You also had to be a union member for two years within television before you would be allowed to work in film as it was a closed shop. I had joined with an eye on the future.

'Later, in the 90s, when I decided I didn't want to be away from home so much, I applied for a Women into Management course, a government-funded BTEC programme at Kingston University aimed at women returners and those needing further training for a step up. It covered all aspects of business management from finance to marketing, human resources (still called personnel then I think) and recruitment. As a result of that I got a job as Video Manager at Artificial Eye and after another few years I was tempted back into production by David Green who had originally offered me my first freelance script supervising job. Again – who you know!'

Sonia Lovett, although no longer with the BBC, is a director/vision mixer/script supervisor/score reader, often doing all four jobs at once, for live multi-camera concerts, opera and theatre, including Garsington Opera.

'It was extremely useful to have been a secretary because the training made me meticulous, organised and efficient: all were essential in my career. I feel really fortunate to be doing a job that I love. I work with delightful people and I am never tired of the excitement I feel when I step into an outside broadcast vehicle or a studio control room.'

Mary Ankrett, whose request to take responsibility for recruitment was originally rejected, found the skills she developed as a PA helped her later when running her own business as a life coach.

'During the 80s I worked for the Chairman and MD of a contract caterer. My boss was more open minded about the role I could play as an assistant, he often asked my opinion and handed over many tasks which he felt I could cope with. I did feel very much a valuable part of his team. I continued to work for him for 11 years. I learnt a lot about business, how it is run and realised one needed more than just shorthand and typing skills in order to do a good job. You needed to be a confidante, understand the business you are working in, have good people and hostess skills and be a travel agent. When I told people what I did, they were impressed. I loved my role, I felt it was important and I was proud of what I had achieved.

> 'I then trained and gained a life coach qualification and started my own business, offering support to a wide range of clients. Everyone is different, every person has different needs and aspirations. Sometimes a person gets stuck in a rut and does not know which way to turn.
>
> 'I am now just over 70, semi-retired. I work as an independent IT tutor, I am deputy chair on a Patient Community and Care Council at the local hospital, as well as a voluntary hospital inspector.
>
> You can be whatever you want to be if you put your mind to it!'

For **Chris Green,** the confidence she acquired from her work at BP led her to other responsibilities, such as becoming a school governor.

> 'I never felt looked down on. I've never thought, "Oh, I am just a secretary". The people I worked for, they always appreciated what I did. I had quite a lot of pride in what I did, yes. And when I eventually retired, I thought, I've spent my whole life helping people.'

Susan Coles qualified as a social worker, a job she enjoyed until she retired. 'As a secretary', she wrote,'you can have a pile of work in the in-tray and at the end of the day the tray is empty and you can go home without any worries. As a social worker there often isn't any closure.'

As one contributor wrote, 'Being a secretary wasn't as easy as it looked.' In my own case, through studying with the Open University I finally got that degree and went on to become an academic librarian. Had anyone suggested to me while I was bashing a typewriter in that upstairs room at Mrs Hoster's, that I would end my working life managing an undergraduate library with a historic archive and a collection of rare books, working with some of the brightest and most interesting young people in the country, I would never have believed them. And, even though I felt trapped as a secretary, the experience I gained from it was of huge value later on. Apart from anything else, it was a useful point of reference when judging what a 'good' boss should do, and it helped me understand the difficulties and frustrations faced by those working at lower levels. And, it's brought me this book. So I have no regrets about my secretarial years and, on a final footnote to them, on the day I retired an email appeared in my inbox with good wishes for my future from the same kind secretary who had taken care of me on that first morning in the Langham.

*****

What remains now of the work that 70s' secretaries carried out? Fifty years have passed, and most of the documents that were so carefully (or not) prepared have long ago been chucked into skips, along with the diaries, notebooks, pot plants, coffee cups, telephones and typewriters that were once essential to every office. A paperless past, perhaps. Was their work valued as much as it should have been? Informally yes but, in general, probably not. And what a travesty it is that this lack of appreciation has continued to blind us to their achievements and left us with glib misrepresentations.

I hope now we can start to redress those misconceptions. Perhaps, if you find yourself in the company of a group of over-sixties' women, it is likely that one or more of them were secretaries in the 1970s. So talk to them. Listen to what they have to say. They may surprise you.

I leave you with these final thoughts.

Jenny Mustoe
London

'Everything needs a support system, whether it's a tiny plant in a pot or a towering building.'

Sue MacCulloch
Middx

'It was a valuable contribution to whichever company you were working for. You're supporting somebody, the boss, and surely supporting somebody is a good thing? It wasn't a dead-end, no-hoper, come-in-and-go-home job. It was purposeful.'

'It was a lovely time: it was a lovely job.'

Sarah Shaw

Acknowledgements

I am very grateful to the following former secretaries who contributed their reminiscences for this book:

Alison Chubb, Amanda Lunt, Andrea Sarner, Anne Ballard, Carol Brinson, Carol Walters, Catherine Preston, Chris Green, Christine Allsop, Claudia Vickers, Corinne Korn, Debbie Maya, Deirdre Hyde, Denise Tomlinson, Diane Jones, Doreen Ashpole, Elaine Day, Elaine Hughes, Frankie Cox, Gill Bazovsky, Gill Perry, Gillian Summers, Gloria Miles, Gwen Rhys, Hazel Channon, Hazel Rees, Heather Harvey, Heather Pippins, Jan Jones, Jane Green, Jane Osborn, Jean Heaney, Judith Farnell, Kate Logie, Kathie Hamilton, Kathryn Baird, Kathryn Vaughan, Laurie McGill, Lesley Powell, Lorraine Oliver, Lucy R. Fisher, Margaret Knowles, Margaret Taylor, Mary Ankrett, Mary L Cryns, Michelle Metz, Olwen Hanson, Pam Robinson, Patricia Robb, Phyllida Scrivens, Rosalind Lee, Rosemary Kaye, Rowena Smith, Sandra James, Sarah Oram, Sharon Tagle, Sheila Shaw, Shirley Cook, Sonia Lovett, Sue MacCulloch, Susan Coles, Susan Strudwick, Susan Weir, Sylvia Dale, Tanya Bruce Lockhart, Terri Kaye, Tina Hawes, Valerie Docker, Verity Lamb, and Wendy Gough.

I am also grateful to the following who helped in tracking down potential contributors:

Natasha MacLean at BBC Alumni, Steve Harris at BBC Radio Solent, Leigh Chambers at Cambridge FM, Roderick Cooper, Elaine Day, Lucy R. Fisher, Jan Jones, Katie Turner, Richard Russell and Dr Schopflin.
At the University of the Third Age (U3A): Francis Beckett, Editor, *U3A Matters*, and the branches in Bridport, Cambridge, Carrick, Edinburgh, Enfield, Nottingham, Scarborough and Sutton in Ashfield.

At the International Association of Administrative Professionals, USA: Adriana Simsen, CAP IAAP Houston, Texas, Karen A. Garrison CAP, OM, IAAP Dover, DE, Vicky Popplewell, CAP, OM, IAAP Arlington, Texas.
The IBM retirees Facebook group, and staff at Kansas City and Vancouver Public Libraries.

Thanks also to the following for information and additional comments:

Anthony Adams, Claire Astbury, Joel Bahl, Kathryn Baird, Mary-Jo Benton, Grace Brown, Ian Burdon, Anna Cassar, Brian Chaplin, Katharine Cockin, Beverly Cohen, Gail Everitt Frankowski Cooper, Sandy Cumming, Susan Curry, Ann Dando, Patricia Delosrios, Christine Donovan, Kathryn Drumm, Elizabeth Edser, Caroline Elkington, Jocelyn English, Catherine Esbester, Gail Everitt, Julie Forsyth, Karen Freeman, Erica Frowd, Dr J. Gilbert, Gothiron, Christina Grimwade, Kate Guest, Jayne Halhead, Lesley Halliwell, Jean Heaney, Helen Heywood, Adam Hickford, Ann Horrell, Elaine Hughes, Diane Hull, Cyn InBelgië, Arleen Jaracz, Rosemary Johnson, Rosemary Kaye, Jayne Kelly, Janet Kingsland, Irene Lavington, Helen List, Elizabeth Carole MacLeod, Verity Martin, Jan Matthews, Will McKinley, Marilyn McLinn, Janet Nicolas, Connie Nolan, Phyllis Ortynski, Gemma Pierson, Linn Rafferty, Rev Duncan Ravenheart, Barbara Rich, Kathleen Hetzler Riordan, Sarah Rudd, Sharon Staples Schulz, Jill Stopps, Hugh Sykes, Carol Walters, Moira Walton, Jennifer Williams, Christine Wilson, Adele Winston, Beth Wishard, Alex Woodward, Jane Zacharzewski, Ems, The Social Justice Paladin, ParmaViolets, Pamela Sunday Handbag and many others on social media.

Special thanks to Robert Gwyn Palmer, Tom Webber at Icon Books and staff at The London Library; and to Sheila Hakin, Deirdre Hyde and Sarah Oram for their help in preparing this book.

Bibliography

Benét, Mary Kathleen (1972) *Secretary: an enquiry into the female ghetto*, London, Sidgwick and Jackson

Cairncross, Frances (1976) *The secretary bird trap*, The Guardian, Sep 27 1976, p.9 ProQuest Historical Newspapers.

Cairncross, Frances (1982) *Sexual blackmailers at work*, The Guardian (1959-2003); Jun 23, 1982, p.10 ProQuest Historical Newspapers.

Campbell, Sir Alan (2004) *From carbon paper to e-mail: changes in methods in the Foreign Office 1950-2000.* Contemporary British History, 18:3, 168-176, DOI:10.1080/1361946042000259369

Carr, Richard, (1974) *The art of making room with a view*, The Guardian, Mar 28 1974, p.17, ProQuest Historical Newspapers.

Carr, Richard, (1974) *Burning desire behind the typewriter to exercise real initiative*, The Guardian, Sep 24 1974, p.10, ProQuest Historical Newspapers.

Cooper, Jilly (1970) *How to survive from nine to five*, London, Methuen.

Coote, Anne, (1972) *With full supporting caste*, The Observer, June 25 1972, p.27, ProQuest Historical Newspapers.

Crookston, Peter & Garner, Lesley *Must the secretary be typecast?* (1972) Sunday Times, 16 July, p.34. Times Digital Archive.

Danzig, Martin E. (1980) *Sexual harassment of working women: a case of sex discrimination* by Catherine A. MacKinnon, Review. The Annals of the American Academy of Political and Social Science, Vol. 449, New Directions in International Education (May, 1980), pp. 204-206
Published by: Sage Publications, Inc. in association with the American Academy of Political and Social Science. Stable URL: https://www.jstor.org/stable/1042153, Accessed: 02-12-2018

Delgado, Alan, (1979) *The enormous file: a social history of the office*, London, John Murray.

Dodd, Celia (1989) *Giving the boss a new secretary bird*, The Guardian, Jun 14 p.21, ProQuest Historical Newspapers.

Dunn, Elizabeth (1971) *Sex and the singular career girl,* The Guardian, Dec 15, p.9, ProQuest Historical Newspapers.

Fyson, Nance Lui (1981) *No sex please, I'm busy: Sexual harassment at work is widespread,* The Guardian (1959-2003); Jan 13, p.8; ProQuest Historical Newspapers.

Gurley-Brown, Helen (2004) *Sex and the office,* New Jersey, Barricade Books Inc. Originally published New York, Avon, 1983. Original copyright 1964.

Office of Population Censuses and Survey. *Census 1971: Great Britain Sample Census, Great Britain, Economic Activity Tables,* London, HMSO, 1974.

Haigh, Thomas (2006) *Remembering the office of the future: the origins of word-processing and office automation* IEEE Annals of the History of Computer, vol. 28 issue 4 pp.6-31.

Hanson, Michael (1974) *Free range in the office,* The Guardian, Mar 28 1974, p.16, ProQuest Historical Newspapers.

Hewison, William (1986) *Funny business: Punch in the office*, London, Grafton Books.

Hicks, Marie (2017) *Programmed inequality: how Britain discarded women technologists and lost its edge in computing*, MIT Press.

Hollowood, Bernard (1978) *Everybody loves temps,* The Observer, Jan 8 1978, p.11, ProQuest Historical Newspapers.

Howell, Georgina (1965) *Our girl Fridays,* The Observer, Apr 18 1965, p.28, ProQuest Historical Newspapers.

Hughes, John C. and May, Larry (1980) *Sexual harassment,* Social Theory and Practice, Vol. 6, No. 3 (Fall 1980), pp.249-280,Published by: Florida State University Department of Philosophy
Stable URL: https://www.jstor.org/stable/23561192, Accessed: 02-12-2018.

Judd, Judith (1982) *When a glance becomes a leer,* The Observer (190-2003); Jun 27, 1982 p.4, ProQuest Historical Newspapers.

Kennelly, Ivy (2006) *Secretarial work, nurturing, and the ethic of service* NWSA Journal, volume 18, number 2, Summer 2006, pp.170-192, John Hopkins University Press.

Kleinschrod, W.A. *The Gal Friday is a typing specialist now,* Administrative Management, vol. 32, no. 6, 1971, pp. 20-27, quoted in Haigh, Thomas, *Remembering the office of the future: the origins of word-processing and office automation,* IEEE Annals of the History of Computing October-December 2006, pp 6-31.

Knight, Kathryn (2014) *Oh for the good old days when bosses spanked secretaries,* Daily Mail, 3 December. https://www.dailymail.co.uk/femail/article-2859918/Oh-good-old-days-bosses-spanked-secretaries-Believe-not-women-say-pine-sexist-office-life-70s.html

Larry (1961) *Man in office,* London, Museum Press

Lowbrow, Yeoman (2015) *Swimming in the steno pool,* Flashbak, https://flashbak.com/ accessed 8 Feb 2015.

MacKenzie, Vicki (1977) *Take a salary of £7,500, Miss Smith,* The Observer, Oct 23 1977, p.26, ProQuest Historical Newspapers.

Man's best friend? (1972) Sunday Times, 4 June, p.68. Times Digital Archive.

McNally, Fiona (1979) *Women for hire: a study of the female office worker,* London, Macmillan.

Miss Smith. "'Take Miss Smith' — Radio 4 looks at the secretary problem." *The Listener,* 19 Dec. 1974, p.815. *The Listener Historical Archive, 1929-1991,* http://tinyurl.galegroup.com/tinyurl/8C9TA8. Accessed 30 Oct. 2018.

Neville-Rolfe, Dorothy (1970) *The power without the glory: the secret of success for sagacious secretaries, enlightened employers and mere mortals,* Literary Services and Production Ltd., London.

Norman, Barry (1973) *Pick of the weak,* The Guardian Sep 24 1973, p.12, ProQuest Historical Newspapers.

Normen, Ken (1976) *Letters to the Editor: Women chained to the typewriter,* The Guardian, 30 September, p.12, ProQuest Historical Newspapers.

'Our Correspondent' (1966) *Days of the shorthand-typist numbered?* The Guardian Feb 2 1966, p.5, ProQuest Historical Newspapers.

Pells, Rachael, (2019) *Are you up to speed?* iPaper, 10 October 2019, p.33.

Peril, Lynn (2011) *Do Secretaries Have a Future?* The New York Times, April 27, 2011, p.27, accessed 30.11.2018
https://www.nytimes.com/2011/04/27/opinion/27peril.html

Peril, Lynn (2011) *Secretaries: glorified servant or canny career move?* The Guardian, 15 September. https://www.theguardian.com/lifeandstyle/2011/sep/15/secretaries-servant-canny-career-move? accessed 30.11.2018

Pitman, Peter (1976) *Now is the time,* The Guardian, Oct 5 1976 p.11, ProQuest Historical Newspapers, ProQuest Historical Newspapers

Polan, Brenda *Separating the sheep from the office goats,* The Guardian, Jan 30 1980 p.11, ProQuest Historical Newspapers

Reed, Christopher (1979) *Degrees of misconduct,* The Guardian (1959-2003); Apr 6, 1979 p.11; ProQuest Historical Newspapers.

Road, Alan, (1988) *Memo to the boss, please help me,* The Observer, Oct 9 1988, p.52, ProQuest Historical Newspapers.

Russell, Diana E.H. (1981) *Sexual harassment of working women: a case of sex discrimination* by Catharine A. MacKinnon, Review. Contemporary Sociology, Vol. 10, No. 2 (Mar., 1981), pp.321-322 Published by: American Sociological Association. Stable URL: https://www.jstor.org/stable/2066977, Accessed: 02-12-2018.

Silverstone, Rosalie (1974) *The office secretary: a study of an occupational group* Thesis submitted for the degree of Doctor of Philosophy, City University London. https://ethos.bl.uk/OrderDetails.do?uin=uk.bl.ethos.472670

Silverstone, Rosalie (1976) *Office work for women: an historical review* Business History, 18:1, 98-110, DOI: 10.1080/00076797600000005

Silverstone, Rosalie & Towler, Rosemary (1984) *Secretaries at work,* Ergonomics, 27:5, 557-564, DOI: 10.1080/00140138408963523

Simons, Violet K. (1966) *The awful secretary's book,* [London], Wolfe Publishing.

British Broadcasting Corporation (2016) *The Dame Janet Smith Review Report.*

Stevens, Auriol (1970) *Girls on a plate,* The Guardian, Feb 20 1970 p.9, ProQuest Historical Newspapers.

Stiernberg, Bonnie (2011) *17 best secretaries in pop culture,* Paste Magazine, May 11. www.pastemagazine.com.

Stott, Mary (1980) *I never expected any secretary of mine to make my tea or coffee: why should I?* The Guardian, March 12 1980 p.9.

Stott, Mary (1973) *The office wife,* The Guardian, Sept 13 1973 p.13, ProQuest Historical Newspapers.

Stott, Mary (1970) *Just a sec,* The Guardian Nov 16 1970 p.9, ProQuest Historical Newspapers.

Truss, Catherine; Goffee, Robert; Jones, Gareth (1992) *Career paths in traditional women's jobs: a comparison of secretarial promotion prospects in England, France and Germany.*
Women in Management Review; 1992; 7, 5; ABI/INFORM Collection p.9

Vinnicombe, Susan (1980) *Secretaries, management and organizations,* London, Heinemann Educational Books.

Watts, Janet (1982) *Secretary birds,* The Observer, Nov 7 1982, p. 25, ProQuest Historical Newspapers.

Webster, Juliet (1986) *Changes in work processes and responses to change with special reference to dedicated word-processing in selected offices in Bradford,*
Thesis submitted for the degree of Doctor of Philosophy, Postgraduate School of Studies in Industrial Technology, University of Bradford.

White, Ann. "The secretary circus." *Sunday Times*, 16 Apr. 1972, p. 7. *The Sunday Times Digital Archive,* http://tinyurl.galegroup.com/tinyurl/8TygB0. Accessed 30 Nov. 2018.

Whitelocks, Sadie (2012) Conical bras, miniscule waists — and VERY SHORT SKIRTS: Daily Mail, 6 September.
https://www.dailymail.co.uk/femail/article-2199344/Flirting-smoking-VERY-short-skirts-Photos-secretaries-Thirties-Swinging-Sixties-reveal-office-culture-decades-past.html

1. Silverstone, Rosalie, *The office secretary,*
2. Silverstone, ibid p.89
3. Coote, Anna, *With full supporting cast*
4. Silverstone, p.133
5. Vinnicombe, Susan, *Secretaries, management and organizations*
6. Hanson, Michael, *Free range in the office*
7. The Guardian 28 March 1974 quoted in McNally, Fiona, *Women for hire*, MacMillan, 1979 p.27.
8. https://www.statista.com/statistics/289158/telephone-presence-in-households-in-the-uk/ accessed 24 Apr 2020
9. Howell, Georgina, *Our Girl Fridays*
10. Gurley Brown, Helen, *Sex and the office* pp.27, 25
11. Parkin, Michael, *Victory for the trouser suits*
12. Silverstone, p.497
13. Silverstone, p.235
14. Silverstone, p.248
15. Frank Muir (1920-1998) English comedy writer, broadcaster and television executive.
16. Dr Louis Marks (1928-2010), historian, television script writer, editor and drama producer.
17. Hollowood, Bernard, (1978) *Everybody loves temps*
18. Silverstone, p.424
19. Silverstone, p.324
20. Norman, Barry, *Pick of the Weak*
21. Benet, Mary Kathleen, *Secretary: an enquiry into the female ghetto* pp..82-87
22. Silverstone, p.427
23. Simons, Violet K. *The awful secretary's book,,* p.42
24. Cooper, Jilly, *How to survive from nine to five,* p.45
25. Gurley Brown, p.33
26. Gurley Brown, pp.185,187
27. Silverstone, p.428
28. Cairncross, *Sexual blackmailers at work*, The Guardian, 23 June 1982 p.10
29. Knight, Kathryn, *Oh for the good old days when bosses spanked secretarie*s
30. Gurley Brown, Helen, p.94, 194
31. Gurley Brown, ibid
32. Now Dame Frances Cairncross
33. Cairncross, Frances *The secretary bird trap*
34. Pitman, Peter *Now is the time*
35. Silverstone, p. 338
36. Dunn, Elizabeth, *Sex and the singular career girl*
37. Stott, Mary, *The office wife*
38. Stott, ibid
39. Gurley Brown, p.6
40. Gurley Brown, p.54

41 Silverstone, p.458
42 Silverstone, p.245
43 *What is word-processing?* (1975) Computer History Archives Project https://www.youtube.com/watch?v=vqTTxLPPE30
44 Kleinschrod, W.A. *The Gal Friday is a typing specialist now.*

Printed in Great Britain
by Amazon